Oil, Pol[itics]
and Seapower
The
Indian Ocean
Vortex

W. A. C. ADIE

PUBLISHED BY
Crane, Russak &
Company, Inc.
NEW YORK

National Strategy
Information Center, Inc.

Oil, Politics, and Seapower

Published in the United States by
Crane, Russak & Company, Inc.
347 Madison Avenue
New York, N.Y. 10017

Copyright © 1975 by
National Strategy Information Center, Inc.
111 East 58th Street
New York, N.Y. 10022

Library Edition: ISBN 0-8448-0617-X

Paperbound Edition: ISBN 0-8448-0618-8

LC 74-29073

Strategy Paper No. 24

Printed in the United States of America

Table of Contents

Preface

This monograph is concerned with the growing involvement of the great powers—the US, USSR, China, Japan, and Western Europe —in the politics of the Indian Ocean area. The emerging confrontation among them suggests that this region will soon become one of the main theaters of conflict in a world already surfeited with political strife and the threat of nuclear war.

The nations bordering on the Indian Ocean—from South Africa to the newly independent states of East Africa, the Arabian Peninsula and the Persian Gulf, the Indian Subcontinent, and Southeast Asia— comprise much of the socalled Third World. Most of this planet's oil resources are to be found here, and a major portion of international commerce traverses the waters of the Indian Ocean. The extravagant wealth of the oil-producing countries contrasts with the poverty and backwardness of most other nations in this strategically vital region. Political instability is a common characteristic. The region is "the scene of continuous guerrilla wars and recurrent conventional wars," and invites the intervention of the great powers, all of which perceive their interests to be increasingly affected by developments here.

Ian W. A. C. Adie's important study focuses on Soviet and Chinese ambitions in the Indian Ocean area, and also surveys the main political and economic problems confronting the various countries of the region. Perhaps the greatest of these is the unattainable chimera of "development"—the consuming ambition to reach the economic level of the Western world, in circumstances where human and material resources are simply inadequate to the task. The result is unending frustration, and growing hostility toward the more fortunate countries of the West. What is really at stake in this region, says Mr. Adie, is the emerging "confrontation between the socalled 'developed' powers

v

and the 'developing' countries"—a confrontation that both Communist superpowers seek relentlessly to exploit in their timeless struggle to overcome the capitalist world.

The author has devoted his life to the study of Asian affairs. After service in Military Intelligence during World War II and postgraduate work at St. Antony's College, Oxford, Mr. Adie served the British Foreign Office at various posts including Saigon, Vientiane, Phnom Penh, and Hong Kong. In 1960, he was elected Research Fellow in Far Eastern Studies at St. Antony's; and in 1970, he was appointed Senior Research Fellow in the Research School of Pacific Studies, Australian National University, where he still is. Adie has published widely on Asian affairs.

> Frank R. Barnett, *President*
> National Strategy Information Center, Inc.

December 1974

1

Great Power Involvement

The two superpowers have beefed up their military strength in the Indian Ocean . . . The scramble for this area between the United States and the Soviet Union will become even fiercer in the days to come. *Peking Review*, January 14, 1972.

The Indian Ocean is of major and growing importance to the developed economic and military powers, but—unlike the Atlantic and Pacific—has none of them on its shores. Inexorably, the great powers and their rivalries are being drawn into an area already racked by poverty and strife. Even before the energy crisis of 1973, the problems of the Indian Ocean posed serious threats to economic stability and world peace.

Growing concern about this area in the United Nations and the countries concerned has been largely deflected from the real issue by concentration on purely military matters. In May 1974, Secretary General Waldheim submitted a report to the United Nations dealing "primarily with the military presences of the great powers in the Indian Ocean area, conceived in the context of great power rivalry." Its conclusion was that a "strategic naval arms race" would ensue if the United States upgraded the Diego Garcia "facility" into a base. This report would seem to be a fitting culmination to previous United Nations treatment of the problems of the underdeveloped Third World, which has usually been characterized by oversimplification, misrepresentation, euphemism, and cant.

1

The Indian Ocean area (which contains much of the Third World) is indeed a focus of international tension. It is the scene of continuous guerrilla wars and recurrent conventional wars. But its troubles do not arise from any danger of a "naval arms race" consequent to the much-canvassed "Soviet naval build-up" and America's projected naval response. These naval activities of the superpowers are froth on the swell. The political furor they helped to stimulate have a great deal more to do with what is really at stake: the confrontation between the socalled "developed" powers and the "developing" countries—a confrontation that has intensified in the context of the energy squeeze and the threatening dearth (or cartelization) of many other vital commodities such as food grains, fertilizer, metals, and even water.

The activities of the Afro-Asian bloc in the United Nations in opposing superpower activities in the Indian Ocean are only one aspect of the present conflict between the more developed countries and their markets and sources of raw materials, and the struggles between the former for the latter, which were envisaged by V. I. Lenin in his theses on imperialism as the final stage of capitalism. Surveying the state of the international economy and monetary system after the impact of the energy and resources crises, even a non-Marxist could be excused for seeing some potential lines of development leading from the present crises to the *denouement* envisaged by Lenin in 1918—"Paris via Calcutta and Peking." To have been really useful, the UN report should have discussed outside military aid to governments and especially to revolutionaries in the area, instead of concentrating on warships.

Published analyses of the possible motives behind the involvement of the Soviet Union, the United States, and other outside powers in the Indian Ocean area seldom take into account that Moscow probably—and Peking certainly— have not only national interests, but also long-term *plans*, in the region. Of course, they are not the only ones; but owing to the different social and political systems of the non-Communist developed countries, the plans that they elaborate are less likely to be coordinated than those of totalitarian societies —although these, too, suffer from bureaucratic and interservice infighting and are not as "monolithic" as they seem.

By limiting the field of vision mainly to military/naval technicalities, it is possible to explain both American and Soviet involvement in terms of defensive moves concerned primarily with the central nuclear balance, and not with the Indian Ocean balance of forces; and to neglect almost completely the influence of China and Japan because of their negligible naval and aerospace power, while assessing their interest—and that of Western Europe—only in terms like "threats" to "sea lanes," "lifelines," and "arteries." But such thinking is at least partly outmoded, because it ignores the new conditions and ways in which these threats are likely to be posed. It ignores the development of weapons technologies and strategy in the nuclear age, the nature of the global, multilevel power game in its present phase, and its superimposition on the internal and external conflicts of the small and middle powers. Above all, it neglects the political-economic dimensions of the manysided power game (sometimes dubbed detente) that has replaced the Cold War.

Since 1968, the USSR has taken advantage of conflicts in the Subcontinent and Britain's withdrawal from "East of Suez" to increase its visible naval activity in the area. Both friends and foes have given this development a disproportionate publicity—which, in return, has enhanced the intended diplomatic effect and diverted attention from the real security problems of the region. Some experts have argued that a sufficient reason for the Soviet naval activity was American deployment of deterrent missile submarines in the area. But it is also perfectly possible that such a policy instrument could be used, if not conceived, to promote Soviet influence in the Third World and so bring on the classical crisis of Western capitalism (especially in Western Europe), while also serving the short-term purpose of encircling and restraining China, pressuring Japan, and preventing a coalition between them.

China may still lack offensive hardware; but its software—heretical Marxism-Leninism, that is, Maoism—is a more dangerous solvent of the erstwhile Soviet bloc than the "sugar-coated bullets of the bourgeoisie." For many years, China has rather successfully contended with the USSR for control of the forces erupting in the Third World in the postwar era of decolonization, "development," and desperation —forces that range in form from pacifism and neutralism, through various expressions of economic and political nationalism, to "national liberation struggles" using the Maoist and Guevarist techniques of "people's war."

On the one hand, China's efforts to win friends and influence people in selected areas of the Indian Ocean littoral (such as Tanzania and Pakistan), and in the Third World as a whole, may be explained away as a counterencirclement against the Soviet drive to "encircle and suppress" Mao's China. On the other hand, Mao and his colleagues could be perfectly serious in their claim to be the true heirs of Lenin—using the slogan of opposition to Soviet (and American) hegemony and the manifold opportunities offered by quarrels and conflicts of interest between them and among all the actors in the international system to manipulate the Third World (and even the developed industrial countries), and thereby contain the USSR and encompass the destruction of "US imperialism and its lackeys."

With relatively modest outlays, and at little risk, Peking's policy to unite the rest of the world against the superpowers has had considerable success, especially since it got into the United Nations in 1971 and greatly expanded the range of its diplomatic and economic contacts. Within the world organization, Peking has worked diligently to "support" resolutions and other agitation by Third World countries on such matters as extension of territorial waters, use of the seabed, fishing rights, peace zones and the exclusion of superpower navies from certain seas, nationalization of minerals and other resources, throwing the US out of Panama, and so on and so forth. In coordination with clandestine activities and people's war at the grass roots level, China's agitation against alleged manifestations of "hegemonism" in the United Nations and similar bodies, and in bilateral dealings with small and middle powers, can to an appreciable extent achieve the same destabilizing results among its targets as more conventional military and naval activity.

China advances the simple and attractive explanation that the Third World's troubles come from "the inequitable international economic relationship imposed on the developing countries by imperialism and colonialism," especially by the struggle between Russia and the

United States to carve up the world between them. There is plenty of evidence that seems to support this thesis, such as the growing gap between average incomes in rich and poor countries, and between the prices of poor country exports and their imports from the rich, industrialized nations. Before the energy crisis, the Chairman of the Bank of Israel's Advisory Committee described this gap (then 3,000 percent) as a "time bomb for humanity as a whole." The energy crisis has now so seriously exacerbated this trend that famine, chaos, and revolution in the Third World are confidently predicted by international civil servants and other authorities concerned with foreign aid and economic affairs. The non-oil producing countries of the Third World located in the Indian Ocean area are said to face a "general deceleration of development" against a background of worldwide recession and inflation.

Even before the energy crisis, a slowdown was expected in the high growth rate of the industrialized nations, with a continuing high rate of inflation. Non-oil-exporting developing countries were expected to suffer a serious deterioration in their terms of trade in 1974-75, due to a levelling out of (and some decline in) the level of commodity prices after very large increases in 1973, along with continuing high imports of manufactured goods from the industrially more developed countries. The combined deficit on current account of the non-oil-exporting developing countries in 1974—excluding the effect of increased oil prices—was forecast at about $14 to $16 billion. The World Bank estimates that, assuming constant volume demand, current world oil prices will increase the oil import bill of these countries from $5.2 billion in 1973 to $14.9 billion in 1974. This is more than the total flow of public development aid to the less developed countries in 1973 ($8–8.5 billion).

In addition to the direct increase in oil prices, the poor countries will also have to pay more for manufactured imports. As recession hits the industrialized nations, prices for the export commodities of the developing countries (such as minerals) will go down as demand shrinks. The combined effect of shortages and high prices for oil and petroleum-based products like insecticide and fertilizer will have disastrous effects on food production and distribution. This will aggravate the existing social unrest.

Even before all this, in 1972, one observer had written in *Harper's* that the "environmental crisis has become the world's most dangerous political issue, as it wrenches back into open view the brutality of racial competition for survival." For various reasons, Latin America will remain relatively immune to these crises. The Indian Subcontinent and Africa (especially Kenya, Ethiopia, Sudan, Tanzania, and Malawi) will be the worst hit. Burma and Indochina will also suffer seriously; and Thailand and the Philippines, which import a good deal of oil, face severe deterioration of their terms of trade. The petroleum crisis has exacerbated the food-grain shortage, which already alarmed international bodies in 1973, because it will lead to shortages and high prices of fertilizers.

The UN technical agencies, such as FAO, have been moving toward the concept of a "minimum world food security policy" involving intergovernmental stockpiling and transfers of food by a system reminiscent of the "ever-full granary" of the old Chinese Empire. China's UN rhetoric repeats that "in the world today, it is the poor countries which feed the rich countries, and the development and prosperity of the latter depends on the exploitation and extortion of the former." In point of fact, the agricultural "developing world" is shown by an IMF survey of May 1974 to be a net importer of food grains—mainly from the US and Canada. These imports are expected to rise from $2.8 billion in 1972 to between $8 and $9 billion in 1974. The World Food Conference (scheduled for Rome in November 1974) was accordingly expected to set up a "world food bank" to mitigate the need for poor nations to tie up reserves in local stockpiles. The trouble is that the UN program will require inefficient and corrupt political regimes to accept and enforce norms of responsible management as far as their circumstances permit. As a report on the FAO's deliberations last year noted with rare honesty:

> There is no doubt that the poverty which is characteristic of many of the world's most populous nations is the result not only of climatic, historical, and social factors, but is in large measure the product of corrupt and inefficient politics.

But this is something that the ramshackle regimes in question are reluctant to admit. It is more expedient to find a foreign scapegoat.

This was the background against which the General Assembly met in April 1974 to discuss raw materials and development. It is worth noting that China sent a top official to this meeting, Vice Premier Teng Hsiao-p'ing. In a rousing speech, Teng expounded the Chinese view that "the whole world is in turbulence and unrest." But this was a good thing. The Socialist camp, he said, "is no longer in existence," the "Western imperialist bloc, too, is disintegrating," and the world today really consists of three worlds—the first comprising the USSR and US, while "the developing countries in Asia, Africa, and Latin America make up the Third World," and "the developed countries between the two make up the Second World."

According to Peking, the superpowers can never reach real detente. "Either they will fight each other, or the people will rise in revolution." So everyone else must join China to defeat the superpowers, some by armed struggle (as in Indochina, Palestine, and Africa), others by the "struggle against maritime hegemony," which the Latin Americans have initiated. Moreover, "the oil battle has broadened people's vision. What was done in the oil battle should and can be done in the case of other raw materials." (Supplement to *Peking Review*, April 15, 1974).

The present "proletarian revolutionary diplomatic line" of the Peking leadership goes back to the Ninth Congress of the Chinese Communist Party (April 1969), at which the late Marshal Lin Piao delivered the keynote report. Premier Chou, usually tagged as a "moderate" by Western commentators, replaced him in this role at the Tenth Congress (August 1973), but Chou's scenario was still substantially the same as the Marshal's famous manifesto of 1965 on people's war and the encirclement of the "world city" by the "world countryside." According to Premier Chou:

> The fundamental principles of Leninism are not outdated. They remain the theoretical basis for our thinking today. The present international situation is one characterized by great disorder on earth . . .

—and, to sum up in plain language, the disorder is caused by the "collusion and contention" of the superpowers, and by other basic "contradictions" between them and the Second and Third Worlds, which altogether are going to bring on world revolution, and so, at last, make the Maoist revolution stick in China.

Out of the "great disorder" of the Cultural Revolution in China came "great order." So it will be with the world. Meanwhile, China has to adapt to the present world situation the flexible tactics of compromise and pseudo-alliance used by Lenin in 1918 and by Mao during his three-cornered war with Japan and Chiang Kai-shek. As Lenin said when he signed the Treaty of Brest-Litovsk in March 1918:

> Maneuvering and retreating is waiting for a new outbreak of the revolution which is maturing in the West . . . we have just one chance until the outbreak of the European revolution, which will solve all our difficulties—the continuation of the struggle of the international imperialist giants.

Peking's media are full of guideline articles and related news items plugging the theme of how this "struggle of the giants" is forcing the Third and Second Worlds into resistance. The latter are setting up or taking over regional and specialized organizations to institutionalize the "struggle" in various "arenas of contention," and even "making it more difficult for the superpowers to monopolize" the UN itself.

Many of the details cited by Peking concerning the "harm" done by Soviet and "imperialist" involvement in intermediate countries are substantially true. The real cause of the trouble, however, is not the "class nature" of the social-imperialists and plain imperialists, which allegedly determines that they must attack and oppress everyone else. It is the myth of "development," that is to say, the all-too-widely accepted expectation that all governments can and must constantly "raise the standard of living" of their population at least to levels approaching those of the most industrialized countries—as measured mainly in material terms like caloric intake, or number of motor vehicles per head, or the use of inanimate sources of energy. There should be no need to labor the point that this is not going to happen. The resources are not available to "develop" Afro-Asian countries in that sense, or even to maintain recent rates of "growth" in the developed countries.

The present monograph cannot digress into the complex question of the "limits to growth" publicized by the Club of Rome and a legion of futurologists. Computer predictions suffer, like the rest, from failure to take account of technical and social innovations unimagined by the programmers. Nevertheless, it is clear that during the remainder of this century, and especially during the next few years (before possible technological innovations can take effect), economic and hence social conditions in the Indian Ocean area will be conducive to the breakdown and fall of governments in the face of civil commotion and war. Because of the dependence of the more developed powers on the region, and especially on Middle East oil, their problems, too, will be exacerbated. It may be noticed that all nine West European EEC countries suffered a change of leadership and/or crisis in government after the energy crisis. Perhaps this was not altogether a case of *post hoc, ergo propter hoc*. It can be argued that the strain which kills statesmen and governments these days is largely due to the fact that they are attempting the impossible.

They are expected to maximize equality among the citizenry—including economic equality—and increase the capacity of the state to cope with its environment, which involves an increasing specialization of institutions and technocrats within the political system. The possibility of meeting the demand for social justice by "natural" means depends on maintaining dynamism (or "growth") in the national economy. But negative economic factors like inflation and scarcity of resources are an *international* phenomenon.

The more a government tries to balance its international payments, raise welfare, and control every variable within its own frontiers, the more dependent it becomes on the world market and other forces beyond its control. As the Chinese say, it is like trying to hold down ten fleas with ten fingers. According to a growing army of pundits, the only answer is to impose "zero growth" and a "constant economy," if not a static "folk society," instead of national states and other goal-oriented, "developing" political associations.

But such well-intentioned calls for farreaching changes in social values clearly foreshadow the transformation of democratic society into a technocratic dictatorship—into modern forms of the ancient hydraulic society, in which absolute authority was legitimized by the need for vast works to control the waters, and to ensure and distribute the crops equitably to a teeming population.

The installation of "efficient" administrations in the Third World at the expense of "national sovereignty" and at the behest of international organizations can indeed be justified in the interests of the ordinary people. But if such a process is accepted widely in the Third World, the already large number of centrally planned economies and politically Byzantine states in the world will increase. Forced to trade and otherwise interact with them, even democratic and "capitalist" countries will have to set up, or increase the role of, state trading and production agencies, counterespionage and security organizations, and so forth.

If China "develops" like Japan, the sheer size of its economy would act as a magnetic field to influence the alignment of the rest of the world. But if the Third World does *not* "develop," and retains its authoritarian yet incompetent leaders, these are most likely to resist international attempts to clean up their stables as neocolonialist interference, and maintain themselves in power by demagogic denunciations of the industrial countries as the real cause of their people's misery. Either way, the Third World, and especially the Indian Ocean countries, are going to be a storm center for the rest of the world, whether on not foreign warships are cruising around their shores.

Moreover, the convenient division of the world into "rich" and "poor" countries, or into three "worlds" in descending order of affluence, is quite misleading. The "Third World" is itself divided into rich countries—especially oil-rich—and the rest, while even the industrial giants of the First and Second Worlds are more and more closely linked with the Third, and are in any case facing similar economic and social problems. As Arthur M. Schlesinger has remarked, "being a leader in any country—whether advanced or undeveloped, a dictatorship or a democracy—is no great fun these days." All industrial societies face intractable problems that the leadership is not capable of coping with. The Malaysian Prime Minister, Tun Abdul Razak, suggested at an ILO conference in June 1974 that the underlying cause of world inflation was "infighting" between the developed countries and a "lack of political will and discipline in important areas of the industrial world." The Conference Board of US economists announced at the same time that the rate of US inflation was a threat to world stability, but attributed it to "a profound historical shift in the social conditions and value systems of democratic capitalism." Modern economic systems, the experts said, are living in an explosion of expectations that carry the demands for output far beyond their finite resources. Dr. Arthur F. Burns, Chairman of the US Federal Reserve Board, warned on May 28, 1974, that even in the United States, "discontent bred by inflation can provoke profoundly disturbing social and political change . . . [and] a significant decline of economic and political freedom for the American people."

In these conditions, the voices that have already been heard calling for a "change" in human values and social systems to avoid ecological disaster are liable to find a growing audience, even in democratic countries. In response to a message signed by 2,200 scientists in May 1971, the Secreary General of the United Nations made the following statement:

> I believe that mankind is at last aware of the fact that there is a delicate equilibrium of physical and biological phenomena on and around the earth that cannot be thoughtlessly disturbed as we race along the road of technological development. This global concern in the face of a grave common danger, which carries the seeds of extinction for the human species, may well prove to be the elusive force which can bind men together. The battle for human survival can only be won by all nations joining together in a concerted drive to preserve life on this planet.

Unfortunately, such hopes for unity in face of a common danger have throughout history been exploited, like demands for equality and fraternity, by the devotees of authoritarianism.

It should be noted in passing that China has the longest continuous and documented experience of any society on earth in dealing with the problems of overpopulation, famine, and social control that now threaten the globe. A plausible case can be made that there is a "Chinese model" of society in which people can be kept quiet *without* too much economic growth or competition—a society in which, paradoxically, inequality and strife are mitigated by the rule of a special caste of dedicated bureaucrats. Because these "cadres" avoid in so far as possible dressing and acting like the ruling class they actually are, many people can be found who sincerely believe that some such system of paternalism is what the world is looking for. It should be remembered that some of the ideological fathers of the French Revolution admired the Manchu despotism of the 17th century. More recent ideas of world government suggest interesting parallels with the model of China as a world in itself, as Mao has rightly called it, and with the government of China—yesterday and today—as a model of world government by soberly dressed international managerial mandarins. Few people would be so inspired by the idea of Soviet-style *apparatchiki* running the world. Peking may have fewer missiles than Moscow or the West, but it has advantages in the realm of ideas and public opinion that may prove important in the long run.

Meanwhile, the increasingly complex pattern of interaction among the conflicting forces in the Third World is generating all sorts of "threats to stability" (1) at the point of production, before the oil, copper, and other resources get near the sea lanes at all; (2) on the transport routes; and (3) at the points of unloading, processing, and distribution in the developed countries themselves. It would be futile for the highly industrialized countries of Western Europe, East Asia, and the Southern Hemisphere to rely solely on the naval and military protection of "lifelines" when they can be cut more effectively and at less cost by a foreign power fomenting and/or manipulating dock, transport, and other strikes, or suitable movements and disorders on their home territory, or nationalism, terrorism, and the like at the producing end.

This study will confine itself to some aspects only of great power interaction in the Indian Ocean area, which do not seem to have been covered fully elsewhere. By "great powers" are meant the US, USSR, China, Japan, and Europe. We shall be mainly concerned with the USSR and China, since Soviet-US rivalry in the area has been widely canvassed.

The US and USSR do have common interests in a sense, but no common borders. The local confrontations of their proxies and proteges have proved cumbersome for their global policy, which is increasingly concerned with China, Japan, and Europe. China and the Soviet Union have both common interests and a highly militarized border. But except for occasional clashes, their conflict has been displaced and "cooled" into a struggle for influence, first in the Third World, and then in Japan and Europe as well. The Indian Ocean comprises the key region of the Third World, which both Peking and Moscow see as the most important arena of their struggle, and in which they have both sought to enlist allies against each other under the pretext of helping them emancipate themselves from the political and economic hegemony of the "West." In recent years, Peking has increasingly denounced the joint hegemony of the capitalist world market led by the United States, and what Khrushchev called the "economic system of socialism" centered on the USSR, and encouraged small and middle powers to emancipate themselves from this dyarchy.

In almost identical language, the militarists of Japan once proposed to emancipate the countries of Greater East Asia from Britain and America. Especially since the fall of Lin Piao in September 1971, China's handling of international relations has increasingly stressed diplomacy rather than "people's wars." But Premier Chou En-lai emphasized in October 1971 that the times still called for "armed struggle" as well as negotiations. This riposte to President Nixon's categorization of the era as one of "negotiations" only should draw our attention to certain historic and domestic factors that have given Mao's China a policy instrument which was not developed—or, at least, not to such an extent—by militarist Japan and the other combatants in World War II, or by the protagonists of the Cold War that succeeded it. This is the "international united front" exploiting existing "contradictions," conflicts, and, in the maximum program, *armed struggles*. In at least three parts of the Indian Ocean area—Africa, the Middle East, and Southeast Asia—armed struggle is sitll very much on the agenda, and has enabled Peking to make gains at the expense of Moscow and other external powers. It must be stressed at this point that, contrary to a widely held theory, Chinese assistance to armed insurgents is not alternative or contradictory to the "normalization" of relations with the governments under attack by the insurgents; it is an inseparable component of the same dual approach. This is attested both by the past theoretical writings of the Maoists and by their present behavior, which will be discussed below.

On the global level, President Nixon expected "a safer world and a better world if we have a strong, healthy United States, Europe, Soviet Union, China, and Japan, each balancing the other, not playing one against the other, an even balance." His Guam Doctrine moves away from the Dulles policy of containment and rollback by means of the "creative counterpressure" of a US alliance system, and toward "creative ambiguity," "benign neglect," and a spontaneous, multipolar balance of power—the counterpressure to China being provided by the USSR, and *vice versa*. Before Stalin's death, the Soviet Union also began to move away from the bloc concept toward Khrushchev's "peaceful coexistence and economic competition." It has recently reached the stage of Dulles pactomania, the minimum program always remaining defense of the revolution (that is, of the ruling group), and the maximum program, its advance (that is, the inclusion of new territory within the Soviet sphere of influence). Beginning with trade and aid (often military, as required by local conflicts), Moscow has sought to promote such "regional cooperation," "economic integration," and "division of labor" as would facilitate the signing of bilateral treaties (as with Egypt, Iraq, and India) and the eventual construction of a collective security system that would render China innocuous by encircling or including it. The Indian Subcontinent is the key to this system, which basically aims to *preserve the status quo*.

China, on the other hand, has recently moved away from the paramilitary approach associated with Lin Piao, and back toward the Soviet-style methods ascribed to Liu Shao-ch'i—conventional state-to-state diplomacy, trade and aid. Its overall economic disadvantages in this field *vis-à-vis* the superpowers have been compensated by certain special conditions in Africa which have enabled Peking to reap great political advantages from the maintenance of a militant posture and the supply of what it had—surplus railway-building capacity, armaments, and other wares less sophisticated than those available from the USSR, but often more suited to African conditions for precisely this reason. Africa has been a key to China's system of the "international united front," which has not sought to maintain the status quo by either an alliance system or a power balance, but rather to generate enough counterpressure to *change* it.

To the extent that China has joined the United Nations and otherwise achieved greatly enhanced world status, it has already broken out of the status quo—the encirclement of the superpowers. But its position is still insecure in many ways. In spite of the military origins and aspect of the Peking regime, China's militancy in Africa and the Middle East must now be regarded primarily as an opportunist tactic in the framework of its policy of mobilizing a "third force" at the United Nations and in the Third World. The support of such a "force" would enable it better to maneuver between its powerful neighbors—the USSR, which constitutes a military and internal security threat; and Japan, which is a threat both as an investor in (and potential ally of) the Soviet Union, and as an extension of "US imperialism," as a long-term competitor with China for raw materials and markets, and ideologically as a giant Taiwan, armed with sugar-coated cannonballs of the bourgeois life-style. Chinese denunciations of a presently nonexistent Japanese militarism are designed not only to head off the possible conversion of Japanese economic power into military and political power, but indirectly to inhibit Japanese commercial competition with China.

In order to understand the importance of the Indian Ocean in the US-Soviet-Chinese global power game, and in the subgames played at each end of Eurasia with Europe and Japan, we need some historical perspective. It is also necessary briefly to consider the problems and policies of the diverse and divided countries of the area which in the past have invited the intrusion of outside powers, and those congruent interests of the latter which may now require them to try and impose some new *pax* upon it. In anticipation, we should note at this stage that although the Indian Ocean has been of marginal importance for the United States (except for the deployment of deterrent missile submarines at a certain stage of technological development), it is already regarded as of major importance for Europe and Japan, and its energy supplies are expected to become increasingly important for the United States itself.

Peking is already exploiting potential US-Soviet competition for Middle East oil. Citing American press reports, the *Peking Review* noted in April 1973 that by 1980, the United States was expected to import up to 50 percent of its oil from the area. The US Committee on Defense Production has forecast that by 1985, 55 percent of US oil requirements would be imported. US naval authorities have specifically adduced this situation as a reason for increased naval activity in the Indian Ocean. In the wake of the energy crisis, the United States made arrangements with Saudi Arabia which *Newsweek* (April 15, 1974) described as a "grandiose aid scheme designed to transform Saudi Arabia into a modern industrial society and a powerful military nation," while also "all but" assuring the United States of adequate petroleum supplies. It is worth noting that South Korea and Taiwan have also made oil deals with Saudi Arabia. While cogent arguments can be marshalled against the idea of crude Soviet interdiction of these supplies, one should note that the companies engaged in extracting and transporting Middle East oil represent 90 percent of the estimated US $2.2 billion invested in the region (excluding Israel). The annual revenue of $1.4 billion from these interests (nearly all of which is repatriated to the United States) is of major importance for the balance of payments.

2

Historical Background

Geography and demography give to the Indian Subcontinent a position of potential predominance in the area that is not paralleled in either the Atlantic or Pacific regions. The area can be seen as the rim of a bowl—the ocean—which is "chipped" at the position of the traditional land invasion route into the Subcontinent. Elsewhere, it is mainly isolated from the hinterland by mountain ranges, deserts, or jungles. Land communications within the region face similar obstacles; hence the past importance of sea communications and sea power.

The ocean has carried commercial and cultural traffic since the dawn of history. In Roman times, the spice trade was as important as petroleum is today. From the fourth century B.C. to the fifth century A.D., Indian shipping predominated; but for the next six or seven centuries, an empire based on Sumatra dominated eastern waters. For centuries, Indonesian emigrants intermittently reached Africa and settled Madagascar. The rise of Islam brought Arabs and Persians on the scene, although Indian writers claim that while Indian kings maintained battle fleets, the Arabs were "only commercial navigators." After the fall of the Abbasid Caliphate, great Chinese fleets—one with 30,000 men—briefly exacted "tribute" from as far afield as Somalia and the Arabian Peninsula. According to the Mauritian historian of the Indian Ocean, Auguste Toussaint, that ocean nearly became a Chinese lake between 1200 and 1433 A.D.; but this maritime, perhaps mercantilist, policy was abandoned as a result of internal conflicts within China.

17

In 1498, Vasco da Gama anchored off Calicut. Within two decades, control of the Indian Ocean had passed to Europe. It was the Portuguese who first practiced the strategy of dominating the ocean by controlling its points of entry. Alfonso d'Albuquerque took Malacca, Socotra, Ormuz, and Goa. Subsequent conquest of Ceylon, Mombasa, and Timor assured Portuguese hegemony in the area through the 16th century. Early in the 18th century, Britain began to emerge as the foremost European naval power, battling with the French during the War of Austrian Succession, Seven Years War, and War of American Independence. Its eventual hegemony over India and the Indian Ocean was due to the exceptional circumstances of Britain's head start over the rest of the world in industrialization. No comparable technological advance had been made, however, in overcoming the land barriers round the area; and this accounts for much of the convential wisdom about Indian Ocean strategy which is still current, if irrelevant, today. Britain's strategic rivalry with France, Russia, and Germany before World War I led to the acquisition of territories in addition to India, notably in the Persian Gulf area and Southeast Asia, which later became of increasing economic importance to Britain but depended largely on India for their security and development. By the outbreak of World War II, it was hard to say whether Britain held the Indian Ocean area in order to secure India, or *vice versa.*

In the interwar period, the main threat to stability in Asia appeared to come not overland from Russia, as in Kipling's day, but from Japanese navel power. After the political division of the Indian Subcontinent in 1947, to some extent China replaced both Russia and Japan as a potential threat to India from the east, whether by land or by sea. K. M. Panikkar's postwar suggestions for Indo-British naval cooperation were ignored by Prime Minister Nehru, however, in favor of his policy of socalled "nonalignment."

With the Soviet Navy and Soviet advisors now increasingly performing the functions once exercised by the Royal Navy and British colonial officials, it is already arguable whether the Soviet military and naval presence in the area is being built up to support onshore political and economic operations, or *vice versa.* Suffice it to note at this stage that apart from Moscow's presumed need to patrol the areas for surveillance of US Polaris or Poseidon submarines (a presumption not entirely borne out by the low ASW capability of the ships so far deployed), the sea area has great potential importance for communications between the European and Asian ends of the Soviet Union, especially in the event of trouble with China and the possible interdiction of the Trans-Siberian railway. The ocean is also a major source of fish, which constitutes an important part of Soviet protein consumption.

Above all, the surrounding land areas are themselves increasingly important economically to the USSR, as well as to Europe and Japan, and political and economic benefits can accrue to Moscow, as they once did to Britain, thanks to the illusion of a "naval presence." Experts may know that such a naval force would be useless in actual nuclear war; but it publicly appears to be—and therefore is—powerful in the conditions of "phoney peace" imposed by the nuclear stalemate, in which manipulation of public opinion and the psychological climate play such an important part. As a UN report on the Indian Ocean rightly points out, naval ships, especially surface ships, are intimidating.

Tsar Peter used to sum up the options in international relations as "make war or do business." For the nuclear age, his successors have blurred the distinction on the premise that total (nuclear) war will be deterred and its aim pursued "by other means," including lower-level conflicts or confrontations conducted by proxy. Khrushchev's Cold War policy of "peaceful coexistence and economic competition" boiled down to a range of techniques for changing the balance of power between the Soviet and Western blocs by first minimizing the influence of other powers in, and then maximizing Soviet economic and ultimately political control over, the contested or less aligned area of medium and small powers under cover of "helping their independence." This was to be done especially by economic linkage and military pseudo-alliances; the "pseudo" element refers to the fact that, as Egypt has complained, *neither peace nor war* were actually meant to break out.

Within this framework, the pattern of Soviet naval expansion has followed four phases. First, exploration of the target sea area by oceanographic vessels, fishing, and merchant ships. Then, short-term visits by Soviet naval vessels for feasibility trials and acclimatization. Next, establishment of a permanent squadron. At this stage, Soviet planners pause to decide what are their priorities (strategic, military, or political), and how best the Navy can help to achieve them. Then they start casting about for shore facilities and other support requirements needed for the operations selected. At present, the Indian Ocean operations have reached this stage.

These naval operations are to be understood within the framework of Moscow's overall policy, one element of which is evidently the result of conflicting pressures for resource allocation within the Supreme Miiltary Council of the USSR. If the Nixon Doctrine has been called a "blue water doctrine," Moscow (like Peking) has also given signs of upgrading the importance of its Navy. Admiral S. M. Lobov, an expert on nuclear submarines, was appointed in 1973 as Assistant Chief of the General Staff, hitherto dominated by the land forces. His Commander-in-Chief, Admiral of the Fleet S. G. Gorshkov, authored a series of articles in 1972-73, in which he implicitly opposed any ideas Brezhnev might have on naval armaments limitation agreements with the United States, and points up the importance of naval power—not only in war, but as a tool of foreign and trade policy, and in relation to use of seabed resources. His emphasis on the need for a navy capable of offensive strategic missions falls within the framework of the general view of the Soviet military services as propounded by Defense Minister Grechko, to the effect that, because of imperialist war preparations, war remains "a grim reality of our time."

While this view contrasts sharply with the "detente" image projected by Brezhnev, it must represent an operational component of overall Soviet policy in the 1970s. In brief, this policy aims at exploiting the fluid and multicentered international situation, not by attempting direct territorial conquest in the first instance, but (1) by gaining economic, industrial, and technical advantages to consolidate the home front through the acquisition of goods and services blindly sold by the democracies in the name of detente and peace, and (2) by achieving psychological advantages throughout the world by promoting moral and physical disarmament everywhere while simultaneously extending Soviet power wherever possible.

In a valedictory statement in July 1974, Admiral Elmo Zumwalt, the retiring Chief of Naval Operations, warned that the US had already lost its supremacy at sea. Others in Washington boast that "the Soviet Union's growing sea power is the US Navy's biggest breadwinner." Under its new head, Admiral Halloway, former commander of the nuclear aircraft carrier *Enterprise*, it is expected that there will be pressure to reverse previous decisions to reduce the carrier force from 15 to 12 by 1980, on the ground that three will be needed to maintain one on station in the Indian Ocean. Added to existing programs, this would give the Navy a lion's share of the military budget, which seems justifiable in view of America's geography.

In contrast to the Soviet pattern, Peking's Cold War strategy, as summarized in 1965 by Marshal Lin Piao, stressed the "intermediate zone" contested by the superpowers. Though Peking seems sincerely to believe in the possibility of a surprise attack by the USSR either on Europe or China, it also recognizes that ideally the Kremlin would prefer to win without a fight, by undermining the enemy's will. Chinese strategy is essentially the same. But because of China's special revolutionary history and present economic weakness, Peking still attributes an important role to Vietnam-type wars, urban guerrilla warfare, and other kinds of small-scale disorder as a means of redressing the balance, although it is also concerned to acquire technology and consolidate the home front with aid from the West and Japan. In addition, it is building up an ocean-going naval force including nuclear submarines and modern surface-to-surface missile ships.

3

Posture of the Indian Ocean Countries: Franconesia and the African States

> The people of Asia and Africa wield little physical power. Even their economic strength is dispersed and slight.
>
> Sukarno at Bandung, 1955.

The Indian Ocean area is neither economically nor socially coherent, nor are many of the states in it. Except for Australia and South Africa, it is poor—both in terms of present income per capita, and in terms of the ratio of population to natural resources. The societies are predominantly peasant (subsistence farming), while much of the soil is infertile and inadequate. Where this is not the case, the territory in question is overpopulated. No country or likely grouping of contiguous countries in the area contains the combination of resources on which the industrialization of a major power such as the United States was based. Only India offers the economies of scale that many types of manufacturing industry require. From this industrial weakness, military weakness inevitably follows.

Such enclaves of modernity as exist within the peasant mass of a given country—plantations, mines, industry—tend to be insufficiently integrated. They play a disproportionately large part in the economy and provide a large percentage of government revenue. Similarly, trade is mainly with countries outside the region. This divorce between the backward countryside and the islands of modernity oriented toward the way of life of "advanced" countries creates manifold social and political problems. In spite of rising expectations, the gap between the "outback" and the Afro-Asian city is expected to increase; so is the gap between those cities and the advanced economies of Europe, the United States, and Japan.

Apart from relative deprivation in material terms, the real cause of the "instability" strategists fear is to be found in the sphere of *psychological deprivation*—for example, frustration of a subelite of young people educated above their parents' level but without satisfactory employment, and of detribalized shantytown dwellers experiencing the industrial revolution. Above all, the rapidly rising proportion of adolescents in the population of many countries has already given cause for alarm. These tensions contribute to the prevalence of xenophobia and communalism in the guise of nationalism, and to merely symbolic development led by a "repainted" traditional elite or a military dictatorship in the name of socialism.

The area divides naturally into seven subregions: Franconesia and the other Indian Ocean islands, Southern Africa, East Africa, the Persian Gulf–Red Sea area centered on the Arabian Peninsula, the Subcontinent with Ceylon, continental and maritime Southeast Asia, and Australasia and Antarctica. The present study will not deal with Antarctica, although recent air activity by South American countries has added an extra ingredient to anxiety already felt in Australia about the future of this continent, of which Australia claims the largest portion. Flights over the icecap to Australia by the Brazilian Air Force and LAN-Chile Airlines, and the Argentine Air Force's plans to build a $14 million airport in Antarctica have raised complex problems of conflicting territorial claims, as well as proposals for internationalization of the whole area under some form of world control.

Franconesia and Other Indian Ocean Islands

I use the term 'Franconesia' to denote Madagascar and three neighboring island groups—the Mascarenes, Seychelles, and Chagos, which were once united under French rule and still retain French connections in varying degrees. In the 18th and 19th centuries, their strategic position made them the scene of naval activity and seaborne commerce centered on Port Louis in Mauritius (then Ile de France), whence expeditions were launched against British India. Diego Garcia in Chagos was occupied by France to forestall a British expedition from Bombay. Britain conquered the islands in 1810, and the first Governors of Mauritius considered it a base for pushing on to Madagascar. But Réunion was left in French hands (as it still is), and France annexed Madagascar in 1895, effectively closing its door to trade and immigration from other islands. This political division of the islands exacerbated their economic decline; although after World War II, commercial shipping revived somewhat and air communications were developed.

Since Mauritius became independent, its Prime Minister, Sir Seewoosagur Ramgoolam, after a visit from Mrs. Gandhi, signed a fisheries agreement with Moscow (1970) which enables the Soviet fleet to replenish at sea and, if necessary, to rotate crews, through aircraft landing rights and trawlers putting into Port Louis. More recently (1972), Ramgoolam visited Peking and obtained Chinese aid for construction of a new airport capable of handling jumbo jets. On the fisheries agreement, Ramgoolam told the press: "We approached Britain, Norway, and Sweden for help, but they were not interested. When the Russians made their offer, we accepted it in good faith. I do not think the military question comes into it." In Peking, and in conversation with the present writer in July 1972, he stressed the problem of unemployment in the island, which is evidently serious. In his view, moreover, the Chinese-built airport would promote tourism.

A Soviet naval force was in harbor during my visit, showing the flag. Of the 25,000-odd Sino-Mauritians, a small number have allegedly been recruited for training in China. Several of the Chinese newspapers published on the island carry Peking propaganda; this is an asset the Soviets do not possess. There can be little doubt that both they and the Chinese, in offering aid, look beyond immediate local considerations to the island's strategic potential, and they are not alone. India and Iran also have it in their sights. Britain maintains a naval communications station at Vacoas, under an agreement which runs out in 1974. There is another station at Mahé in the Seychelles. Recently Iran, which is developing a navy to replace British power in the Persian Gulf and to operate in the Indian Ocean, successfully approached Mauritius for facilities. (Iran's policy will be discussed in the next chapter).

The importance of Mauritius has from time to time been enhanced by proposals that British arrangements involving the naval base at Simonstown in South Africa be replaced by Port Louis. This idea, favored by President Nyerere of Tanzania and the former Mauritian Foreign Minister, Gaetan Duval, could not be realized owing to Britain's policy of strategic retrenchment. Under the Simonstown and Sea Routes Agreements of 1955 covering the transfer of the base to South Africa, the British government incurred legal obligations concerning combined naval operations, supply of naval armaments, and the like, which have given rise to much controversy because of South Africa's apartheid policies. The dismissal of Duval in December 1973, along with other ministers of the creole and pro-French *Parti Mauricien Social-Democrate*, was seen in Paris as a serious blow to French plans for a possible French naval base in the island. The immediate use of a naval base in this area would be for surveillance and protection of the Mozambique channel between that territory and Madagascar, which is used by supertankers plying from the Middle East to Europe and the Atlantic.

In 1965, Diego Garcia ceased to be a dependency of Mauritius, and was joined with Aldabra, Farquhar, and Desroches of the Seychelles to form the British Indian Ocean Territory, in order to afford a defense facility in the area for Britain and the United States. While a source of great fuss, this is not yet a "base" of any sort, although some naval planners would like it to be. It is a military radio station, part of the network which includes Kagnew in Ethiopia and North Cape in Australia. If US plans for upgrading the facilities there come to fruition, there will be a 12,000-foot airstrip capable of handling KC-135 and B-52 aircraft (though there is no official intention of using the latter there), and facilities for naval ships to moor and take on spare parts and the like.

Apart from "bases" properly socalled, there are a number of other facilities—ranging from access to ports and airfields, to communications installations—dotted about the Indian Ocean, on islands and on the mainland, many of which are shared by more than one ex-

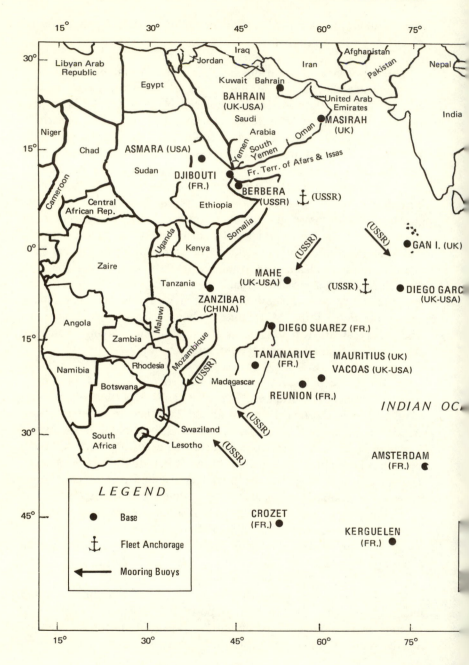

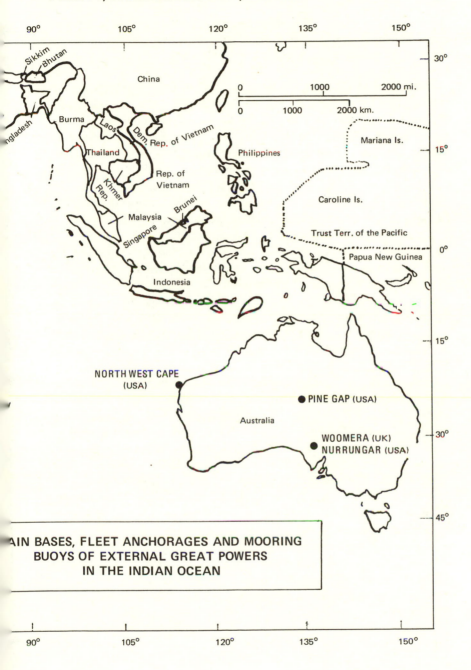

MAIN BASES, FLEET ANCHORAGES AND MOORING
BUOYS OF EXTERNAL GREAT POWERS
IN THE INDIAN OCEAN

ternal country. They make an impressive show on a map if all are indiscriminately called "bases" or "base facilities." But this is an abuse of language, often intentionally misleading.*

"Bases" in the normal sense can be said to exist in Diego Suarez (Madagascar) and Djibouti, where France has naval facilities, and at Gan in the Maldives and Masirah Island off Oman, where Britain has air staging posts. The Maldives opened diplomatic relations with Peking last year, as did the Malagasy Republic following student demonstrations in May and the replacement of President Tsirinana by General Ramanantsoa's regime. The Comoro Islands, site of another naval facility at Mayotte, are also due to win independence from France. Mayotte has an excellent deepwater bay.

Ultimately, the stability of Franconesia is largely dependent on what happens in Madagascar, the potential "hyphen" linking Asia with Africa. Local sources discount the likelihood of China having promoted the May 1972 troubles—though it gained from them, as it did previously in Zanzibar. The student movement was fueled by genuine grievances against the educational system, which was geared to produce unemployed BAs, and other aspects of the excessive French influence in Malagasy culture and commerce. But the background is more complicated. The students were backed by the leading trade union body, FISEMA, which is affiliated with the Soviet-controlled World Federation of Trade Unions and closely linked with the "Kim" (AKFM, *Parti du Congrès de l'Indépendance de Madagascar*), a Moscow-oriented group linked to the Réunion Communist Party. Kim's claimed membership of 25,000 is largely confined to the capital. Despite appearances, this movement is essentially an elitist reaction of the Merina or Hova ethnic group of Indonesian origin, whose domination of the coastal African tribes ended when the French conqueror Galliéni freed the slaves in 1896. The Merina inhabitants of the capital and surrounding plateau are mostly Protestants, converted by British missionaries in 1840-60. The coastal Africans are largely Catholic. With some reason, the latter see the overthrow of their kinsman President Tsirinana as a restoration of Merina rule.

---

* For details on existing bases and other facilities, see the three appendices in the back of the book.

The riot that toppled Tsirinana and the PSD (Social Democratic Party) was precipitated by arrests of students on the night of May 12, and firing on the resulting demonstration by the FRS (Republican Security Forces). This praetorian force had been built up as a counter to the Army by André Resampa, Secretary General of the PSD, a former Vice President, and the designated successor to Tsirinana until his arrest in June 1971 on trumped-up charges of plotting. Tsirinana had remarked: "If the Army goes awry, I shall always have my security forces." But with the FRS neutralized in its barracks by public execration, he was forced to hand over to the Army on May 18. General Ramanantsoa, of St. Cyr and Indochina, released Resampa and other "plotters" and agitators, including Monja Joana, the "Maoist" leader of the Monima Party, which was implicated in a peasant uprising in the south in March 1971.

The first results in foreign policy were announced in June by Foreign Minister Didier Ratsiraka: "reappraisal" of intergovernmental cooperation and dialogue with South Africa, and of the postindependence treaties with France. *Inter alia,* this meant shelving South African projects for investment in Madagascar, and a setback to Pretoria's policy of "dialogue" with the independent African countries. Significantly, Peking stepped in (January 1973) to replace South African capital in one investment. More importantly, it meant asserting an independence from France which had hitherto been too nominal for the liking of the younger generation.

Diplomatic recognition was also switched from Taiwan to the People's Republic of China. Internal politics since installation of the military-technocratic regime have been characterized by demagogic activity on the part of the revolutionary students, the AKFM, and other groups, each vying with the other to demand nationalization of foreign enterprisees, suppression of foreign bases, and so forth. An agreement with the Malagasy government required the French to withdraw their Legionnaires, parachutists, and naval and air detachments from Diego Suarez within two years (1974-75). Since the energy crisis, however, and its spectacular arms deal with Saudi Arabia, France has created a new naval command extending from Djibouti to the Kerguelen Islands in the Antarctic, and from the West African coast to Sumatra and Malaysia. The new Commander-in-Chief, Rear Admiral Jean Schweitzer, operates from a floating headquarters, *La Charente*, and disposes of a sizable force, including the nuclear submarine *Le Redoubtable*, which is equipped with Polaris-type missiles.

The French Diego Suarez base is, of course, on the coast and the population is *ipso facto* not enamored of the Tananarive "progressives." The military regime has been at pains to deny any intention to restore Merina domination under cover of a People's Democracy; the province chief of Tuléar, at the other end of the island, assured the southerners that the government was "purely Malgache, run by people from all 18 tribes." It is significant, however, that all existing village and quarter chiefs were to be replaced.

The final result of the Malagasy Republic's delayed "completion of independence" may be to bring Soviet involvement with the Protestant elite once favored by Queen Victoria, and China's involvement with their Catholic former slaves. On the African continent, the two Communist superpowers have notoriously backed rival "liberation" groups with essentially tribal differences, while denouncing each other for splitting the movement.

Southern Africa

The burning issue in Southern Africa is generally thought, thanks to years of anti-apartheid agitation, to be that of racial oppression, that is, of "blacks" by "whites." Mirroring the archaic and oversimplified attitude of some right-wing Afrikaner nationalists, a broad spectrum of Pretoria's critics from Western liberals to the Peking government lump together all whites and all blacks with varying degrees of well-meaning ignorance, hypocrisy, and self-serving mendacity. In fact, the area contains several distinct "tribes" of whites and many of blacks, some of whom have in the past "oppressed" people of their own color. Is it necessary to recall that treatmnet of the natives was an issue in the original conflict between the Boers and British; or that before settlement of Rhodesia, the Shona were "oppressed" by the Ndebele? Such factors are still relevant to the present day—Afrikaners politically dominate the English-speaking

South Africans; the Rhodesian situation is different from that of South Africa; and that of the Portuguese different again.

In reality, internal racial conflict as such is not the issue in Southern Africa. The rules of socalled "petty apartheid" may add to the misery and injustice that accompanies industrialization under any system, but they are observed and enforced less and less; and the Africans, on whose increasingly skilled work and purchasing power the system must depend, are getting more and more of both.

The Chairman of the Anglo-American Corporation of South Africa, Harry Oppenheimer, reported to the Royal Institute of International Affairs (London) in May 1974 that "after 26 years of National Party government, there are practically no English-speaking South Africans in leading positions in government, or in the civil service, or the armed forces, or the police, or the government-controlled corporations." The rapid economic development of South Africa was proving incompatible with the government's racial policies.

It has been calculated that if the Gross National Product is to grow at the rate of five percent a year, a rate which is absolutely essential if the new workers entering the labor market are to be absorbed, there will by 1980 be a need for 3,500,000 workers in skilled occupations. Of these, not more than half and probably considerably less can possibly be white.

The prospect of independence for the Bantustans, starting with the Transkei, is another factor whose significance does not yet seem to have struck the general public outside South Africa. In March 1974, Paramount Chief Kaiser Matanzima introduced a bill in the Legislative Assembly of the Transkei calling for independence within five years. He rejected comments in the Assembly that the Transkei would take its land claims against South Africa to the United Nations after independence.

Industrial unrest in South Africa may be given racial overtones, but the real problem is state-to-state relations between the "white" south and the "black" countries sandwiched between it and the Arab north. These are becoming increasingly committed to support for movements which purport to "liberate" the south, but which in fact threaten their black hosts more than the whites. In some cases, these movements aim at the reconstitution of precolonial patterns of empire across the present arbitrary borders—for example, the Kongo Empire, divided in the colonial era between the French, Belgian, and Portuguese areas.

Since the early 1960s, the Chinese have considered Africa as a key area, both because of its plentiful resources and its various "contradictions" awaiting exploitation. In April 1964, the *Peking Review* carried several articles on Africa *à propos* the projected Second Afro-Asian Conference. Africa, it wrote, "is an important economic base for the very existence of West European and North American imperialist and colonialist countries . . . Because of its geographical position and its many strategic minerals and raw materials, Africa holds a vital place in the war and aggression plans of the imperialist camp . . . Africans who want to win and sustain independence are left no choice but to take up arms." The same issue carried attacks on the Soviets as false friends of freedom fighters and as opposed to war, and correctly noted that it "has become the practice of the leadership of the Soviet Union to try to convert international democratic organizations into mere instruments of Soviet foreign policy." At that time, Liu Shao-ch'i and his associates were engaged in trying to create a parallel system of pro-Peking Communist Parties and international organizations to beat the Russians at their own game; the Second Afro-Asian Conference due to be held at Algiers would have added the keystone to this edifice, and consecrated China's leadership of a Third World united front forged in actual "struggles" —"many Vietnams"—especially in Africa.

Today, in spite of two changes of leadership in Peking, its view of Africa is much the same. *Peking Review* wrote in December 1972 that "the gold, uranium, diamond, and copper deposits in Africa occupy an important place in the world . . . rice and natural rubber produced in Asia make up more than 90 percent of the world's total. [Hence] the Asian-African-Latin American region is where the two superpowers contend with each other in their bid for world hegemony . . . [Colluding and contending with the United States,] Soviet revisionist social-imperialism takes pains to set up a network of bases extending from the Mediterranean, the Red Sea, and the Persian Gulf (Arab Gulf) to the Indian Oceon, turning this area into its sphere of influence. Moreover, it is carrying out expansion in the Pacific . . . Following the old imperialist 'gunboat policy,' Soviet revisionist social-imperialism is sending its fleet to the Mediterranean, the Indian Ocean, the Pacific, and the Atlantic in a bid for world hegemony."

The same issue reports the normalization of relations between China and Zaire—an event that symbolized the great shift in China's policy toward Africa after 1970. To a considerable extent, the United Nations itself, the Organization of African Unity, and other world bodies fulfill the function for which Peking had previously tried to employ the Afro-Asian People's Solidarity Organization, the "Second Bandung Conference," Sukarno's "newly emerging forces" (NEFO), and the rest. African states form one third of UN membership. Chinese guideline articles on Africa through 1973 and 1974 continued to harp on the primary importance of "armed struggle." *Peking Review* of January 26, 1973, for example, welcomed the decision at the Eighth Summit Conference of East and Central African Countries that "the armed struggle is the only way through which colonialism, apartheid, and racial discrimination in Southern Africa and Guinea (Bissau) can be eliminated."

Originally, Peking supported rebels against independent African governments, as in Cameroon, Niger, Zaire, and elsewhere. But Rhodesia's Unilateral Declaration of Independence provided a perfect target for "struggle" against this African "Israel," in much the same way that Arab guerrilla organizations in the Middle East, supported by China, were formed ostensibly to fight Israel, but then openly declared the necessity of overthrowing existing Arab governments first.

The idea underlying this strategy is the application on the world scale of the methods used by the Chinese Communist Party in its three-cornered warfare against Japan and Chiang Kai-shek. The basic trick is simply to win over a target group by provoking strife with a third party, and then posing as—indeed, really acting as—an indispensable ally against this "enemy." Variants of the pattern include the artificial "provocation of imperialism" by demonstrators, guerrillas, and the like, to force a counterattack on the target group with exploitation of genuine preexisting "contradictions" (conflicts), the radicalization and subtraction of the supporters from under a "friendly" leader (united front from below, or drawing off water to catch the fish), and the coopting of the leader in order to get at his people or troops (united front from above). The common factor is the presence of a "main enemy" as the catalyst of change or, as the Maoists call it, after Herzen and Lenin, "revolutionary algebra."

East and Central Africa, the Horn, and Egypt

In Peking's view, the strategic key to the African continent is Central Africa, to which the access is via Tanzania and Congo (Brazzaville) and nearby islands. The manifold "contradictions" to be exploited range from internal tribalism and racism and the economic and administrative weakness of the recently-independent regimes (30 coups in 15 years), to the manifestations of these problems on the international level. These often take the form of tensions and conflict between Muslim and non-Muslim (mainly Christian) groups along the cultural/religious "fault line" that crosses the continent from Nigeria through Chad and the Sudan to Ethiopia. Until recently, southern Sudanese Christians allegedly received support from Israel and Ethiopia in their struggle against the Islamic north, while the Muslim Eritrean Liberation Front received help from Arab countries and China in their guerrilla war against their Ethiopian Christian rulers, who were also threatened by Somali shiftas and irredentist claims sympathetically publized by Peking.

In the past, Communist China was not averse to supporting armed action by former slave owners against their former victims, as in Rwanda and Burundi. Peking has benefited from the pressures exerted by such opportunist "deviations" to establish or improve diplomatic and trade relations with Ethiopia, Rwanda, and Burundi, on President Nasser's principle that "the squeaky wheel gets the grease." After the Emperor of Ethiopia's visit to Peking in October 1971, China and Sudan reportedly cut off aid to the Eritrean Liberation Front. In 1972, Chinese technical teams arrived in Ethiopia to study projects for a proposed $80 million loan. In September 1972, an official of the Organization of African Unity in Addis Ababa stressed that China's influence was now "overwhelming." Another highly placed Ethiopian joked that the trouble with Addis Ababa was "slavery in town and cannibalism in the suburbs." Several such people clearly saw the liberation of Africa as starting with the overthrow of the "Imperatore" in Addis itself. The revolt of February-March 1974 and the subsequent deposition of the aged Emperor were hardly unexpected.

From Peking's point of view, the "principal contradictions" in Africa should now be between all the northern and central African countries against the "white" south. Until recently, Israel's success in wooing some African states such as Uganda, and various civil wars with a "Muslim vs. the rest" aspect, had prevented the junction of the two theaters—Islamic Africa *versus* Israeli "Zionism," and Black Africa *versus* "racial discrimination" in the white south. Colonel Qaddafi of Libya has bridged this gap to a considerable extent; Uganda and several other African countries have now broken relations with Israel, while China's entry into the UN, and its extension of bilateral relations with many formerly hostile African countries such as Senegal, Cameroon, and the Malagasy Republic, have created a new situation. Now, Peking can not only manipulate both the "Zionist" and "racist" issues to win Arab and African allies on the ground and at the expense of the US and USSR, but also use them to manipulate the UN and other international bodies.

This gain for Peking is likely to be enormously increased by the opening of diplomatic relations with Zaire and the visit of President Mobutu Sese Soko to Peking. Though the President's motives can only be guessed at, from Peking's point of view a vital "connection" has been made across the waist of Africa, closing the geopolitical gap between two long-time radical pro-Chinese "territories."

Chinese aid to Tanzania and Zambia for construction of the Tanzam Railway has to be seen in a global context, that is, along with its quantitatively comparable aid to (West) Pakistan (linked to China by the all-weather Kashgar-Gilgit highway since February 1971). Ancillary programs and military aid to the regular forces, militia, and ostensibly antiwhite guerrillas in the railway-building countries must also be taken into account. The long-term political purpose of the railway is to facilitate the severance of economic ties between Zambia and other countries north of the Zambesi with the south, in the context of an escalating confrontation that will impose the same break by military and political means. Because of technical factors, such as the inadequacy of the port of Dar-es-Salaam even after completion of the railway, economic factors alone will not suffice to cut off Zambia from the outlets it will probably still need through Rhodesian and former Portuguese territory. However, political tensions and violence across the borders of Tanzania and Zambia continue to increase. The Chinese encourage the formation of, and train, paramilitary youth movements, militias, and guerrillas in order to neutralize the regular security forces, which might otherwise move to seize power before the "united front" process has gone too far, as happened in Indonesia, Ghana, and several other countries.

The general idea behind Peking's original commitment to the Tanzam Railway and related projects is conveyed in parable by the famous revolutionary Peking opera sponsored by Madame Mao, entitled "Taking Tiger Mountain by Strategy." A Chinese Communist squad infiltrates an enemy-controlled area, helps the local "masses" get a railway running to build up their economic and hence military strength, then leads them in an assault on the enemy stronghold— which an agent has penetrated in disguise, winning the confidence of the "bandit" leaders. With the fall of Lin Piao and his militarists, however, the signs suggest that Peking is now less interested in eventual armed conflict, and more in the "complete,"—that is, *economic* —"emancipation" of African countries. This means cutting their existing trade relationships, preventing the expansion of trade with Japan, and linking them to China instead under the banner of revolutionary solidarity and "antihegemonism."

In July 1972, Tanzania's Minister of Commerce announced that China had replaced Britain as the country's greatest source of imports. Press reports have alleged that a Chinese advisor sits in the import licensing department of the Bank of Tanzania, in order to ensure that only items unobtainable from China are imported from elsewhere. Under the railway agreement, 52 percent of the costs are to be defrayed by the local sale of Chinese goods, not to be repaid until 1983. Concern has been expressed in Zambia, Tanzania, and even Kenya that this maximization of Chinese imports was hurting local industries. Local sales resistance has also caused a serious backlog in sales of Chinese goods by the governmental distribution systems and private enterprise smuggling into Kenya. Nevertheless, the image created by China's state-to-state aid remains excellent, particularly in contrast to that of the Soviets. As a result, China has increased its influence not only in Ethiopia (where the process is at an early stage), but also in Sudan, Somalia, and in Egypt and other Mediterranean countries.

Somalia is still Moscow's main foothold in the strategic northwest of the Indian Ocean. Following a $40 million Chinese loan in 1971, however, the President of Somalia visited Peking in 1972. Things also moved ahead in Sudan. After Moscow's involvement in the attempted Communist coup against Nimeiri, the Sudan strengthened relations with China as well as with the West. In May 1974, General Nimeiri diversified his options by downgrading revolutionary socialism and encouraging investment by Saudi Arabia, Kuwait, and other Arab oil countries at the instigation of a well-known Saudi millionaire, Adnan Khashoggi. But initially, China took over training of the armed forces from the expelled Russians, and supplied a complete brigade of tanks and eight MiG-17 aircraft. General Nimeiri and his Chief of Staff, General Khalafallah, said publicly that the Russians had used the supply of spare parts for their arms as a "pressuring tool," and always tried to plant their advisors in nationalist armies, whereas the Chinese did not.

In the same vein, a group of distinguished Egyptians, including members of the original Revolutionary Command Council, memorialized President Sadat that it was "time now to reconsider the policy of extravagant dependence on the Soviet Union . . . the policy of alliance with the devil is not objectionable—until it becomes favorable to the devil." Sadat dismissed the Russians and sought help from China and Europe; but adequate replacement of Soviet weaponry proved unavailable, mainly for technical reasons in China's case and political in the case of Europe. Ultimately, Egypt too moved West; and in March 1974, Cairo signed major concession agreements with US companies to search for oil and gas in Egypt. This trend was confirmed by President Nixon's visit of June 1974 and his offer of nuclear technology to both Egypt and Israel.

It was clear that Russia's presence in Egypt was primarily meant to arm and use Egyptian forces for Soviet purposes in the Mediterranean (such as surveillance of the US fleet), rather than for Egyptian purposes *vis-à-vis* Israel. The same sort of intention was to be seen in Soviet involvement in Iraq and Iran, the two Yemens, and both India and Pakistan.

But China has an intangible advantage over the USSR in the Middle East because of its more vociferous support for the radical guerrilla movements. Similarly, China has recently restored its links with resistance groups in Africa, challenging Soviet influence where it was predominant and supporting rival splinter groups not favored by the OAU or Moscow. China's efforts are now directed primarily against the Portuguese territories and Rhodesia. While helping small movements like COREMO, ULIPAMO, and PAPOMO (intended to form a nucleus of a Mozambique Communist Party), Peking has also equipped FRELIMO with most of its weapons, including assault guns and antitank launchers. Since the visit of an MPLA delegation to China in 1971, this traditionally Soviet-sponsored Angolan movement has also received Chinese training for its personnel. During 1973 and 1974, Peking media reported with satisfaction the increased military activity of the MPLA, FRELIMO, and PAIGC, and also stressed the merging of ZANU and ZAPU, the resumption of armed attacks by "the Zimbabwe people" on Rhodesia, and the decision of the OAU Summit Conference in May 1973 to intensify the armed struggle.

It is clear from the Chinese coverage that the main importance lies not in the real or exaggerated fighting on the ground in Africa, but (as in the case of Vietnam) in the disruptive effects *elsewhere in the world* of protests and propaganda exploiting the gut issues of "racism," antiwar sentiment, and "anti-imperialist struggles."

The most recent example of the results may be seen in Portugal. Although the coup government of General de Spinola associated itself with the exiled Socialist leader Mario Soares and the Communist leader Alvaro Cunhal, by May 1974 its position was already threatened by the activities of the largely Maoist MRPP (Revolutionary Movement of the Proletarian Party). The MRPP used the standard techniques of seizing unoccupied flats to house shack dwellers, exploiting workers' agitation to purge managers for "fascism" and take over industries, and covering walls with slogans urging troops to desert, demanding arms for the "people," and denouncing the junta as an instrument of the bourgeoisie. Alarmed by the influx of self-appointed ultraleftist advisors and propagandists from Italy, Germany, and France, General de Spinola reportedly asked the "revisionist" Cunhal to help keep the Maoists under control. But in September, de Spinola was forced to resign.

At one end of the scale, there are local plots, demonstrations, and riots; at the other end, the Chinese media have made the most of international events such as the Security Council Meeting at Addis Ababa in January 1972, the Ninth Conference of OAU Heads of State and Government at Rabat in June, and the anniversaries of Africa Liberation Day (May 25). During the Addis meeting, Foreign Minister Chi P'eng-fei sent a message to Secretary General Waldheim stating that the people struggling against racial discrimination "should be given energetic moral, political, and material support by all countries that uphold justice." Another Chinese statement said, in part: "In order to uphold the purposes and principles of the UN Charter, the UN should actively support the just struggle of the people of Southern Africa . . . and condemn the South African Rhodesian and Portuguese colonialist authorities, and the US, British, and other governments which support them behind the scenes." Taken with China's demand that the UN Charter itself be revised and "the status quo changed," this and similar statements confirm Peking's hopes to enroll the United Nations and the Organization of African Unity in its effort to internationalize and institutionalize its "united front" techniques.

4

Posture of the Indian Ocean Countries:
Arabia, the Persian Gulf, and the Subcontinent

The Arab people's struggle against aggression and control is now merging with the struggle of the Mediterranean countries to drive out the US and Soviet fleets . . . with the struggle of the Gulf countries to free the area from the superpowers contention, and with the struggle of oil-producing countries in the Middle East to defend national rights and interests. *Peking Review,* January 12, 1973.

Arabia and the Persian Gulf

The above quotation shows how Peking would like to link up various "struggles" separated geographically—on different parts of the chessboard—as well as "struggles" on different functional boards, such as the economic, political, and submilitary (for example, the guerrillas in Dhofar and Palestine). During the visit to Peking in March 1965 of a Palestine Liberation Organization delegation led by Ahmed Shukairi, it was stressed that "first and foremost, and even more important than the reconquest of Palestine, is building its capability of encircling and subduing the ultrareactionary rightists, the bourgeois royalists, and the pseudo-Socialists of the Arab states, and to sweep away all these vermin."

The six-day war of June 1967 gave new opportunities for China and its allies to discredit Arab governments, including those supported by Moscow. Dr. George Habash, leader of the Popular Front for the Liberation of Palestine (PFLP), said in an interview that after 20 to 30 years of struggle, "not only will Palestine be free from Zionism, but Lebanon and Jordan will be free from reaction, and Syria and Iraq from the petty bourgeoisie. They will have been transformed in a truly Socialist sense, and united Palestine will be part of a Marxist-Leninist Arabia." In a similar vein, Nayef Hawatmeh, leader of the Popular Democratic Front (PDFLP), said that turning the battle against imperialism into a popular armed struggle could only be effected by turning the Arab region into a second Vietnam, with a continuous struggle against "imperialism, Zionism, and all agents and reactionary classes." Since the Palestinians in Lebanon and elsewhere are emphatically not local "fish in the water," but more in the position of foreign intruders themselves, a generalization of disorder would indeed be essential for their success. The Maalot massacre of May 1974 is an example of action taken to prevent resolution of the conflict. If the settlement of June 1974 holds, China and the extremists will be able to exploit the dissatisfaction of many Arabs. It is against this background that China and the USSR have maneuvered to exploit the dangerous problems of Israel and the Arab-Islamic world. In practice, Sino-Soviet rivalry has been intense in both South and North Yemen, with respect to the "liberation movements" in Arabia and the Gulf, and in the field of state relations in the Gulf itself.

The importance of Socotra and the Gulf of Aden lies in their control of one entrance to the Indian Ocean, while the significance of the Arabian Sea lies in its proximity to Soviet targets for submarine-launched missiles. It is also a potential outlet to the Indian Ocean both for China (through Kashgar-Gilgit-Karachi), and for the USSR (through Afghanistan, via Kandahar-Quetta, or possibly via a separatist Baluchistan to Gwadar or the Iranian port of Bandar Abbas; according to some reports Gwadar is being improved with Soviet help).

In North Yemen, the Soviets built a port and the Chinese a road. Both contributed to the overthrow of the Imam's government, for which Egypt is usually held to be mainly responsible. Indeed, the leader of the coup was the colonel in charge of the port, Abdallah as-Sallal. A recent study observes: "The amount and dispersal of [a] Chinese loan [to Aden] suggests that China may well play in South Yemen the economic role played by the USSR in the north. It would be naive not to regard the 300-mile road [toward Muscat and Oman] as a strategic path to revolution in the same sense as was the 227-kilometer road of North Yemen in 1962." Soviet military aid to both Yemens predominates. The Soviet radio *Peace and Progress* commented that Peking bragged about friendship with the Yemeni Republic, "but when we seek for concrete expressions of this friendship, Peking has nothing to offer but Mao Tse-Tung's Thoughts."

It is precisely Peking's "software" or ideological approach, however, which has been able to ensure that Soviet hardware is used to China's advantage. China's support for the Dhofar rebels (later PFLOAG) persuaded the USSR also to assist the destabilizing efforts of the rebels of the Gulf, against its interest in maintaining good relations with Iran and Iraq, and in securing Gulf oil for Eastern Europe. In the long term, the insurgency in southern Arabia, which has already caused incidents across the Empty Quarter in Oman, may seriously threaten Saudi Arabia and Gulf oil. The guerrillas are supported by the DPRY government in Aden, which is the most radical in the Arab world.

The Aden government has refused to recognize the independent United Arab Emirates set up by Britain on its withdrawal from the Gulf, and it is likely to continue support for subversion in the area, with Communist backing. Although China has pragmatically opened relations with Kuwait and Iran (on the Mediterranean board), it also retains its revolutionary aims and credentials, and is closer ideologically to the DPRY leaders in Aden than the Soviets are. Like other Chinese-oriented countries, South Yemen is developing a people's militia (to counterbalance the regular armed forces), apparently initially trained by China. (Reports from Teheran in May 1974 suggested that Cuban advisors have now displaced the Chinese.)

According to reliable sources in Teheran, the Shah of Iran, in recognizing Peking and sending his Queen there in 1972, had much the same object in view as the Emperor of Ethiopia—removing Chinese support from domestic and regional dissidents and more importantly, adding a "Chinese card" to the fragile edifice of the regional balance of power.

The net result of China's gains in the Mediterranean and Middle East area in the early 1970s was, paradoxically, an increase in Soviet involvement in the area. While signature of the Soviet-Egyptian treaty of friendship in May 1971 was counterbalanced by President Sadat's purge of "leftists" under Ali Sabry and the subsequent moves to reduce Egyptian dependence on Soviet advisors, the similar Soviet-Iraqi treaty of April 1972 was accompanied by a Soviet naval visit to the Gulf and Kosygin's official opening of the Soviet-aided Rumaylah oilfield. *Le Monde* commented that the treaty was aimed at preempting Chinese penetration of the Gulf as the British withdrew. Note should also be taken of Moscow's agreements on technical cooperation with Iran, and for supply of natural gas to the USSR.

Fearing Iraq, and the disintegration of Pakistan under Indo-Soviet pressure (which would affect its own Baluchi border area), Iran has been rapidly expanding its military and naval forces, with the result that senior Indians have expressed fears of a "new Moghul Empire." The July 1973 coup in Afghanistan and the irredentist "Pushtunistan" policy of the new regime aimed at Pakistan, automatically aligned Kabul with Moscow and Baghdad against Peking and Islamabad. An enlarged Afganistan actually incorporating the Pushtu areas of Pakistan would have access to the sea, however, and thereby would presumably be less dependent on the USSR. Moreover, if India could push up to the Indus, it too would have no reason to depend on Moscow, as at present, for support against Pakistan and its allies. Of course, a reconciliation among Pakistan, India, and Bangladesh could achieve the same effect.

The partial rapproachment among these states has already opened the way for Iranian diplomatic moves in this direction. India and Pakistan settled their differences over Bangladesh in April 1974. In June, shortly after the Indian nuclear test and its offer of a SALT-type treaty to Pakistan, both India and Pakistan moved to modify the status of their respective portions of Kashmir. (The next step would be to devise linkages between the two more autonomous halves of the territory.) In this environment, the Shah activated a longstanding plan for some kind of Indian Ocean economic community. After the energy crisis of 1973, Iran pushed hard with offers of aid and oil sales to India and Afghanistan on special terms. In March 1974, Zulfikar Ali Bhutto visited Teheran to seek assurances that Pakistan would not be bypassed, and came away with concessionary oil sales and promises of aid worth US$ 500 million. At the ECAFE session at Colombo in the same month, Iran offered $678 million (Australian) in aid to a dozen countries of Asia, Africa, and Europe. In Fall 1974, the Shah visited India and Australia, reportedly with the purpose of promoting bilateral economic relations and his projected grouping. Thus, Iran's growing involvement in the Indian Ocean is not merely a matter of military build-up (though this also is impressive), and may well contribute to a settlement of the problems of the Subcontinent, including Kashmir.

At present, however, the serious economic problems of India, and Bangladesh, and their continuing political divisions keep the superpowers involved. The Soviet operation in India provides a useful model of how Moscow would like its bilateral relations with countries such as Malaysia and Indonesia to develop, and ultimately to coalesce into the collective security system mooted by Brezhnev in 1969.

The Subcontinent and Sri Lanka

Here, the "principal contradiction" is expressed in the form of "fissiparous tendencies"—communalism or local nationalism exacerbated by religious differences, and institutionalized up to the state level by the existence of Islamic Pakistan and now (paradoxically) secular Bangladesh. The political divisions of the Subcontinent have enabled outside powers to pick proxies in the area and indigenous factions to select protectors, resulting (broadly) in Pakistan's alignment with the US (against communism in the US intention, but against India in Pakistan's), and later with China (both against India and the USSR), and now India's alignment with the USSR against what is perceived or projected as a joint US-Chinese threat. In the Middle East, Moscow has diversified its options by dealing with Egypt's rivals, Syria and Iraq. In the Subcontinent, too, it has supplied arms to Pakistan as well as to India. Moscow has also tried, as far as possible in view of the prime commitment to India, to push regional economic cooperation so as to link both countries with the Soviet economic system, and to build them up, with Bangladesh, to "contain" or balance China. This balance must be thought of as ultimately military in the sense of preventing a redeployment of Chinese troops to the northern Soviet border, as well as affecting more intangible factors such as economic power, Afro-Asian leadership, and Soviet influence in the United Nations.

Meanwhile, Mrs. Gandhi has sought to balance Soviet influence by mending fences with China, but Peking has shown no eagerness to reciprocate. Allegedly, this was because of the hostilities between India and Pakistan and the subsequent retention of Pakistani prisoners-of-war by India. The same reason was also given for China's initial veto on the admission of Bangladesh into the United Nations. A more compelling reason for Peking's attitude was the likelihood that if it had responded to Indian overtures, Pakistan would have felt obliged to reinsure with Moscow. With Soviet political influences strong but lacking the same lasting economic base (for example, a grain surplus) as American influence, a Chinese *political* counterbalance and a "Western" *economic* counterbalance was indicated. But this realignment took time to eventuate.

With right-wing elements from the splinter Congress group joining Mrs. Gandhi's ruling party, her dependence on the Communist Party of India (CPI) was reduced. Moscow accordingly encouraged the CPI to step up agitation against the government, leading the *Times of India* to speculate that Moscow was seeking to end its "more or less complete identification" with New Delhi. This "identification" seems to have originated from Soviet hopes of taking over the idea of regional economic cooperation, first mooted by India during the period of China's Cultural Revolution, and building on it Brezhnev's edifice of "collective security."

Moscow has pushed its own version of collective security on three levels—economic (cooperation), political (treaties), and military, the latter being the submerged part of the iceberg. Initially, it was necessary to concentrate on the economic stage, so as to draw in Pakistan. (Suspecting these implications, perhaps, Peking commented that the efforts of "the Indian reactionaries" to form an anti-Chinese alliance had to be carried out "under the camouflage of economic cooperation . . . Indira Gandhi made a big effort to peddle the idea of 'regional cooperation' in Asia, pretending that the countries of Southeast Asia should stand together and help one another in becoming economically strong in order to deal with the socalled threat from China.") The 1971 crisis enabled Russia to move onto the political level with India, implementing plans laid in 1969. Article 9 of the Indo-Soviet treaty provides that if "either of the Parties is attacked or threatened with attack, [they] shall immediately start mutual consultations with a view to eliminating this threat and taking appropriate measures to ensure peace and security for their countries." It has been suggested that Indian antisubmarine warfare forces might, therefore, be used against US Polaris/Poseidon submarines in the Arabian Sea or Bay of Bengal. India is reported to have offered facilities (not "bases") to Soviet warships at the submarine base of Vishakapatnam, where Soviet naval aid is concentrated, and at Bombay, Cochin, Marmugao (Goa), and Port Blair in the Andaman Islands, from which ports Soviet missile submarines could operate against China.

The Indian Navy has been supplied with Soviet submarines and other equipment, giving rise to the problem of distinguishing a Soviet-manned Soviet warship from an Indian one. In spite of much fuss about Soviet "bases," similar to the furore over Diego Garcia, official investigations have concluded that "the USSR is seeking only limited berthing and recreation facilities in the region, although undoubtedly it would wish to keep its options open for the future." A recent study of Soviet naval policy concludes that:

> The presence of the Soviet Navy in the Indian Ocean is *so far* not large enough or supported on a scale sufficient for farreaching *naval* objectives. It probably represents a combination of flag-showing force and area-familiarization detachment oriented (a mix of SSM, SAM, and ASW ships) to an anti-Polaris and/or anticarrier role, *with the additional political objective of securing denuclearization of the Indian Ocean.* (Emphasis added).

It would be ironic if the naval option recommended to India by K. M. Panikkar in 1945 were exercised on behalf of the USSR instead of in connection with Britain and its natural successor, the EEC.

India has, in fact, strongly supported proposals for neutralization of the Indian Ocean and its recognition as a zone of peace, first made by the Lusaka Conference of Nonaligned Countries in September 1970 and by Mrs. Bandaranaike of Sri Lanka (Ceylon) at the Singapore Conference of Commonwealth Heads of Governments in January 1971. One of the reasons for Sri Lanka's preference for such a solution is the role of the Indian minority within the island's multiracial structure, which forecloses the option of regional security arrangements implying Indian hegemony.

Here again, the oil-rich states of the Middle East are likely to play an important role in altering the balance of forces, not only in the military sphere, but in economic aid and political influence with impoverished countries such as Sri Lanka and Bangladesh. It was largely thanks to Middle Eastern influence that Bhutto brought off his reconciliation with Sheik Mujib at the Islamic Summit in Lahore (February 1974). A Calcutta journalist commented that New Delhi could not base its foreign policy on "the abstruse concept of secular socialism, which can have no meaning in a country whose illiterate peasants survive through their personal entrepreneurial skills and are sustained by their faith"—Islam. After the reconciliation between India, Pakistan, and Bangladesh (April 1974), and India's request to the United States to renew food aid a few weeks before, the balance of forces in the Subcontinent was clearly more satisfactory than immediately after the 1971 war.

While advocating the peace zone as an ideal, Sri Lanka has in practice followed a "more the merrier" or balancing policy toward the involvement of big powers in the region. Colombo maintains better relations with China than with the USSR (there are not many Overseas Chinese in the island), and has also extended a welcome to US naval forces. Persistent reports about Soviet or Chinese hopes for a "base" at Trincomalee are officially discounted. When Soviet forces got a foot in the door on the pretext of defending the government against the JVP rebels, they were soon sent off again by Mrs. Bandaranaike.

5

Posture of the Indian Ocean Countries: Southeast Asia

The "principal contradictions" in Southeast Asia consist in Balkanization and minority divisions. The problem of the Overseas Chinese in effect reaches up to the state level in Singapore, which is regarded increasingly as a sort of Chinese "Israel" surrounded by the Malay-Muslim world, all the more suspect because of its potential links with China. On the other hand, with the end of the Indochina War already declared and perhaps one day realizable in fact, some observers in the area, especially Singapore, fear that the North Vietnamese Communists rather than China will be a seriously destabilizing element in the region. This would be particularly so as they seek hegemony on the Indochinese peninsula in order to strengthen their state against China, the hereditary enemy.

From the point of view of the great powers, Southeast Asia is a vital link and transit area, and also possesses great, partly untapped natural resources. On November 16, 1971, Indonesia, Malaysia, and Singapore issued a statement to the effect that the Strait of Malacca was not an international waterway, though fully recognizing the right of innocent passage by international shipping. The implication of this, taken with a claim for a 12-mile limit for territorial waters, is that the Sunda and Lombok Straits could also be denied to the Soviet fleet, cutting communications between the Baltic and Black Seas and Vladivostok for about six months of the year. China's vociferous support for measures taken by several countries to extend their territorial waters may be due to the fact that there are over a hundred straits which are "high seas" when the limit of territorial waters is three miles, but instead become "territorial waters" when the limit is twelve miles. The Malacca Strait is one of them.

Indonesia also has a neutralization concept applicable to Southeast Asia only. The aftermath of the 1965 coup in Indonesia and the end of *Konfrontasi* enabled, indeed required, the Soviet leaders to reappraise their policy toward Jakarta, and *vice versa*. The decimation of the Indonesian Communist Party imposed on Moscow the tactics of the "united front from above," with the government instead of from below; but attempts to make "fisheries" agreements and the like as the price of renegotiating outstanding debts made little progress in face of the anticommunism and pragmatism of Indonesia's military rulers, who were not greatly interested in reactivating the rusty Soviet-supplied fleet built up by Sukarno, but who were deeply preoccupied with their Overseas Chinese and other factors of disunity.

While the military in particular are concerned with the possible effects of "playing the Chinese card" on internal security, civilians tend to see some value in it, if only to "follow the trend." Ambassador Soedjatmoko, for example, has written:

> China may well have a stake in an increased self-reliance of the countries of the region. At some point, she may even come to see the utility to her of some nonideological form of regional cooperation, aimed at enhancing regional strength and self-confidence. And with some stretch of the imagination, it may not be entirely inconceivable that China at some point will see the advantage to her of a system of interlocking external balances in the region which, in combination with the increased capabilities of the countries themselves, would amount to *an effective neutralization she may not even be asked to guarantee.*

For while China was placing its stones over the last few years in Moscow's back yard, the Middle East, during the late 1960s the Soviets and other East European countries reciprocated by opening diplomatic relations with Malaysia and Singapore, and developing trade or other contacts with Thailand and the Philippines. Soviet naval activity was also increasing, and Soviet divisions were massing on China's frontier. All this added up to the "creative counterpressure" or shock treatment necessary to persuade China to "join the world." This set the stage for an approach similar to that of the Shah in the Gulf—seeking to give both Russia and China a stake in one's stability. At the same time, regional cooperation was developing with the creation of ASPAC (June 1966), ASEAN (August 1967), the Asian Development Bank, and other regional institutions.

As Adam Malik, Indonesia's Foreign Minister, has pointed out, the three basic options for the countries in the region are neutralization; alignment with one or a combination of powers; or, preferably, development within the region of an area of indigenous stability, based on indigenous social, political, and economic strength. President Suharto has chosen the latter option, which he calls "promoting the national resilience of the respective nations."

> If this can be enhanced to *regional resilience*, then we can be sure that the stability and security of this region can be preserved by the nations of the region themselves. However, the concept needs time to materialize . . . Through the national resilience of each country in this Southeast Asian region, the concept of the neutralization of Southeast Asia will possibly be realized in its true sense, and *not merely* be *neutralization* dependent on the big powers. (Emphasis added).

Malaysian ideas of regional security are closely connected with considerations of internal unity and security arising from the disparity between the economic and political power of the local Chinese community, and the shadow cast by China itself over the region. As Tun Abdul Razak puts it, "the China issue is at the center of Malaysia's foreign policy."

How to give China a stake in the stability of multiracial Malaysia? On the one hand, direct dealings with Peking are expected to head off the possible development of "Chinese chauvinism" orienting loyalties outside the country, and to deprive its extreme expression, the jungle Malayan Communist Party guerrillas, of Peking's support. On the other hand, direct monopolistic trading by the Government Trading Corporation, PERNAS, with its Chinese counterpart should help to prevent the economic strength of the local Chinese and their links with China from having a disruptive effect.

Tan Sri Ghazali Shafie proposed the neutralization of Southeast Asia at a Preparatory Conference of Nonaligned Countries at Dar-es-Salaam in April 1970. Later, three preliminary steps were listed as necessary before the superpowers and China could in practice guarantee it. Each country must set its house in order, develop a "greater sense of regional consciousness and solidarity," and "demonstrate that our activities and policies do not adversely affect the basic legitimate interests of the major powers." Failing this, Malaysia continues to rely on the Five-Power Defense Arrangement until it can safely be phased out.

This is understood by policymakers in Indonesia and Singapore, who have privately expressed doubts about the feasibility of Malaysian-style neutralization. Singapore would naturally regard the exclusion of outside powers as implying a Malay/Muslim hegemony and encirclement which could be dangerous in the event of leftist radicalization or revolution in Indonesia or Malaysia. It therefore inclines to the "more the merrier" approach, on the ground that the great powers cannot be kept out of the area anyway. As Lee Kuan Yew has put it, "we must . . . be realistic, and expect there will be considerable competition for influence among the major powers over this region." What is not clear, Singaporeans say, is why China *should* help Kuala Lumpur solve its communal problem.

In spite of much talk since November 1971 about the enlargement of ASEAN and the neutralization of Southeast Asia, practical problems such as the Sabah issue between Malaysia and the Philippines blocked progress. Another factor may have been a certain conceptual confusion about the meaning of neutralization as distinct from neutralism, nonalignment, neutrality, demilitarization, disarmament, the declaration of "peace zones," pacifism, and so forth. It is worth pointing out that the term "neutralization" refers to a precise status which can only be based on an international agreement, of which the prime example is Switzerland. Its status as a neutralized state in both peace and war was laid down by the Act of Paris of November 20,

1815, signed by Austria, France, Great Britain, Prussia, and Russia as guarantors of Switzerland's perpetual neutrality and the inviolability of its territory. In return, the neutralized state is obliged to eschew foreign military aid, bases, and the like, or any kind of alliance. For this reason, Switzerland is not even a member of the United Nations.

On the other hand, the status of a "neutral" or "nonaligned" state (such as Sweden) is proclaimed unilaterally and would appear to operate only *ad hoc* for a given conflict or period of time; there is no legal obligation by outside powers to guarantee or defend it, or by the "neutral" state to avoid outside military involvements in peacetime. Politicians have not always observed these fine distinctions. A Malaysian minister, for example, wrote that neutralization "refers to the act which brings about a state of neutralism, [which] refers to the foreign policy of a state, either alone or in concert with other states, in time of peace."

Neutralization in the proper sense could hardly be acceptable to Indonesia, or to Singapore, apart from the tie-up with China, which begins with the valid argument that the guarantor must be an outside power, but then may slide over to the notion that China *must* be involved *in* the area diplomatically and in other ways, or even ultimately as a member of some new regional grouping.

The Australian Labor government has shown a tendency to associate the ideas of modifying existing regional security arrangements, and of neutralization and "peace zones" in Asia and the Pacific, with the active involvement of China in the region. But soundings along these lines by Prime Minister Whitlam were not welcomed in Jakarta or New Delhi. As for the Soviet Union, after initially scoffing at the idea of neutralization, Moscow tried to use it as a starting point for its own collective security scheme, presenting the Malaysian proposals in *Izvestiya* as "repercussions" of Brezhnev's. The Soviet government organ was unusually explicit in stressing the relationship between collective security and the "social liberation of the Asian countries, and the liberation of their economies from the overlordship of foreign monopolies."

For the long-term future, Chinese policy toward Southeast Asia will evidently depend, to a considerable extent, on whether China will be able to compete with the USSR, and perhaps Indonesia, in exporting its own oil—with political strings; or whether it will be necessary, as a second best, to make itself a "force to be reckoned with" by the petroleum-importing countries, by using such means as (1) support of guerrilla movements, and/or winning over in various degrees the governments of the area, or (2) by the direct deployment of naval strength, as in the Paracels incident.

At present, China regards itself as self-sufficient in oil production —because its consumption *per capita* is extremely low. The USSR and COMECON, on the other hand, are already suffering from an increasing gap between Soviet production and COMECON requirements, which makes it inevitable that Moscow should solicit help from both Japan and the United States in developing the Tyumen oilfields in Siberia and the necessary pipelines to the Pacific coast, as well as developing Iraq as its window on the Gulf and simultaneously importing gas from Iran. If only to offset the political effects of such Soviet economic linkages, China must logically keep alive the interest shown by petroleum circles in both Japan and the United States in developing its offshore oil, although it probably has no intention of allowing any direct foreign participation in drilling or production.

In June 1973, a senior official of the Ministry of Foreign Affairs in Peking played down the possibility of China developing oil exports in order to pay for the large amounts of modern technology it has been talking about with foreign corporations. Supply of the million tons of low-sulphur crude already sold to Japan has created rail transport and other problems. The development of additional oil resources would take time; and in any event, the oil would not run away. China was still a predominantly agricultural country.

Despite this modesty, the official was probably aware that his technical colleagues had already begun negotiating with Japan and several Western countries for the purchase of self-elevating drilling barges, a pipeline from the Taching oilfields in Manchuria to the port of Talien (Dairen), and many other items of equipment for development of China's onshore and offshore oil industry. One drilling barge had already been bought in 1972 to operate in the shallow Gulf of Pohai; and the year before, refining capacity had been raised 16 percent and crude production 27.2 percent with equipment from ENI (Italy) and SNAM (France). During late 1973 and 1974, the Peking media carried an increasing number of success stories about the oil industry; and in January 1974, Chou En-lai told visiting Japanese Foreign Minister Ohira that output of crude in 1973 reached 50 million tons—about 70 percent over the 1972 output. This made China the eleventh largest oil producer in the world, and marked its emergence as an exporting country. A few days before, a *New China News Agency* report revealed that "large-scale construction of new oilfields was undertaken in several areas this year. A number of new oil wells have gone into production . . . There are also bright prospects for petroleum on China's continental shelf."

Even with the new Manchurian pipeline and the improvement of loading facilities at Talien and other ports, in the immediate future China will not be able to supply more than about two days' consumption of petroleum per annum to Japan. On the other hand, the export of even three million tons per year would have considerable symbolic value as an earnest of future possibilities. Token deliveries to smaller consumers like Thailand, the Philippines, and Hong Kong have also had an appreciable propaganda effect.

Effects of the Yom Kippur and Bangladesh Wars on South and Southeast Asia

The net result of events in the Subcontinent since the energy crisis and the Bangladesh War has been to reduce the reasons for Indian dependence on the Soviet Union and for Pakistan's ties with China. Paradoxically, the explosion of India's nuclear device in May 1974 tended to enhance both these results in the long run. Professor V. P. Dutt of the University of Delhi has commented that "India will not accept decisions from outside, including the Soviet Union." Alleging an "element of intimidation" had entered the picture, Pakistan temporarily broke off talks with India about the restoration of travel and communications. On the other hand, important factors maintained the trend away from polarization in the Subcontinent. In the short term, India's social and economic crisis dictated its appeal to the United States to renew food aid. In the long term, "going nuclear" (even in a backhanded manner) reinforced the widely held view expressed in the January/April 1974 issue of the authoritative Delhi journal *China Report*: "By virtue of her size, location, population, and economic strength, India is the natural big power in the area and cannot shun for long a role appropriate to her size and strength." The author of the article notes that Iran's military buildup is not backed by indigenous industry, and suggests that Iran's involvement with Pakistan is to be explained only in terms of Gulf oil politics. Hence, Iranian ambitions "need not be taken too seriously." The other Indian Ocean countries are not in the running. "The giant harbor, and the finest naval base of Britain in the prevacuum days, at Trincomalee, is now in a state of torpor. To keep one destroyer escort, nine gunboats, and one tug in such a fine harbor is like keeping a sack of wheat in a modern silo. The situation in Singapore and Aden is equally bad." The article concludes that India must build up its economic strength and its Navy, starting perhaps with the merchant marine, and also develop its undersea resources. The significance of recent (May 1974) reports of oil strikes and of potential US participation in exploration off India's coast may help to determine whether this scenario is ever acted out.

Meanwhile, according to one report in the *Far Eastern Economic Review* (June 3, 1974): "Indian strategists are contemplating the development of a nuclear-powered submarine and a fleet of at least 20 to 25 oceangoing submarines. There is a proposal to spend Rs. 10,000 million for a ten-year plan of naval development, including missile ships, and half that sum on the Air Force." (This would amount to US$1,219.5 million for the Navy, and half that again for the Air Force). Another scenario is suggested by Professor Ashok Kapur in the March 1974 issue of *World Today*. Arguing that China no longer perceives India as a pawn in the Soviet game, he concludes: "It is now possible for both powers to bypass the effects of the 1962 war and to recognize the need to combine tacitly against the superpowers. Such tacit coordination suggests that the India-China relationship was already structured before the 1962 crisis, and that policymakers can resume it now, leaving academics and legal experts to decipher the causes of the war." Professor Kapur follows trends of thinking among policymakers in New Delhi. Commenting on the significance of India's nuclear test, a member of this influential group stated recently that although there were wide differences of opinion on some aspects of future policy, nuclear development was an effective unifying factor providing a sense of purpose and dynamism which, it was felt, India had lacked hitherto. Moreover, the program would inject a need for efficiency, and therefore a pretext for expanding the private sector, cutting down the nonsense of post-office socialism and diverting funds from superfluous projects ("the edifice complex") to growth-promoting uses. Above all, the program would show "the superpowers that they can't push us around any more." According to Professor Kapur, "the option which is emerging is the one voiced by Mr. Whitlam . . . [namely,] that regional rather than international powers should manage the movement towards peaceful change in Asia." The key word here is *manage*. Will China and Japan allow India to "manage" the Indian Ocean region when all three countries are propelled by internal forces to flex their muscles in the international arena?

Another possible challenger to Indian supremacy is Indonesia, a country with a remarkable maritime tradition. Unlike India, Indonesia has greatly benefited (at least initially) from the oil crisis. In 1974, Indonesia's crude cost US$16.20 per barrel on a posted price of $19, as against less than $6 in 1973, before the Yom Kippur War. Instead of a balance of payments surplus of about $600 million in 1974-75, Indonesia will now have a surplus of somewhere between $2.25 and $3 billion. Thus, even while import prices rise sharply and revenue from other exports like rubber, timber, tin, palm oil, and spices remains depressed, there will still be a huge surplus.

However, social conditions indicate that this economic input may blow the fuses instead of being usefully absorbed. The population of 130 million is growing by 2.6 percent per annum, and adding 1.2 million a year to a "labor" force which already consists largely of underemployed and unemployed people, including high school and university graduates. An adequate cadre of competent officials and professional men is lacking to turn the cash into generalized "development." The 3.5 million Chinese play an essential part in running trade and commerce, and so earn unpopularity and accusations of corruption for the government as well as themselves. The hostility touched off by visible inequalities in the distribution of wealth has erupted in recurrent pogroms, as on the occasion of Prime Minister Tanaka's visit, and demonstrates the continuing potential for "people's war" techniques in Indonesia.

One result of Indonesia's improved economic position has been acceptance by the USSR of its claim to a 12-mile limit on territorial waters and to the archipelago principle, in furtherance of a one-year trade agreement (signed March 1974) and the proposals made by Deputy Foreign Minister Firyubin on Asian collective security during his visit earlier in the month. The agreement provided for large Soviet purchases of Indonesian rubber. On strategic issues, Firyubin advocated "open sea" status for the Indian Ocean. Asked if the Soviets would withdraw naval forces if the United States did so, he replied that "this matter should be reached later in the process of detente." On collective security, Indonesian Foreign Minister Malik said that "we do not want to reject the idea, but it is still not clear to us." However, the regional trend toward rapprochement with Peking reinforced arguments in favor of reinsurance with Moscow.

The effects of the oil crisis on the Philippines and the creaky countries of continental Southeast Asia—especially Vietnam—are expected to be serious, compounding their existing problems of insurgency, communal strife, and social agitation (Burma, Thailand, Malaysia, Philippines), and full-scale "people's war" (Vietnam, Cambodia, and Laos). While Japan has hitherto been the looming external presence in the political-economic sphere, the new situation has given China an opportunity to combine oil diplomacy with stepped-up guerrilla warfare in the region. The symbolic deliveries of petroleum to Thailand and the Philippines contributed to domestic pressures which were in any case moving the leaders of the Southeast Asian countries, and especially Malaysia, in the direction of closer diplomatic ties with China—with Indonesia and Singapore reluctantly bringing up the rear.

Shortly before Tun Abdul Razak's visit to Peking to see Mao and open diplomatic relations, Ch'in P'eng's Malayan Communist Party, which has been increasingly active since 1968, carried out its biggest terrorist operation in 15 years. The Voice of the Malayan Revolution commented on the Razak visit to Peking that: "Beset by external and internal difficulties, the Razak clique now has no alternative but to follow its imperialist masters in making the socalled readjustment to its China policy." About a year before, the MCP had threatened that the new highway linking the states of Perak and Kelantan would be attacked; and in an attack on May 23, 1974, 68 pieces of roadbuilding equipment worth US$6.28 million were blown up. On the one hand, there was an element of truth in the Communist radio's charges about internal difficulties, in that Razak's visit to Peking was partly motivated by the desire to improve the government's political standing among the Malaysian Chinese as well as to cure the "siege mentality" of the Peking leaders. On the other hand, Peking's failure to dissociate itself from the continuing terrorism left uncertain the possibility of other neighboring states following Kuala Lumpur's lead.

The most glaring apparent evidence of inconsistency in Peking's policy was the assassination of Malaysia's Inspector General of Police, Tan Sri Abdul Rahman Hashim, on June 7, 1974, a week after Tun Razak was feted in Peking; this was the culmination of a series of assassinations of Special Branch antiterrorist personnel by the MCP. In the hope of discouraging the jungle terrorists, the Malaysian authorities dropped photographs of the Malaysian Prime Minister being received by the Chinese leaders. But Peking media such as the pseudo-clandestine Voice of the Malayan Revolution had already provided against such moves. After the Cultural Revolution of 1966-69 and the implementation of the new "revolutionary diplomatic line," various intrumentalities such as the VMR, the Voice of the People of Burma, and the Voice of the People of Thailand were set up in China so that the Chinese government could receive delegations from these countries in a friendly manner, and make references (for example) to "Malaysia," while the pseudo-clandestine stations went on broadcasting coded messages to the guerrillas, denouncing the Malaysian government, and continuing to refer to "Malaya" and calling East Malaysia "North Kalimantan"—the point of the term Malaysia being to stress the unity of continental Malaya (West Malaysia) with the North Bornean territories.

The North Kalimantan Communist Party, an apparently separate organization active in Sarawak, had published a statement in the *Peking Review* and other Chinese media in April under the significant heading, "Continue Along the Road of Seizing Political Power by Armed Force." It said, in part:

> We Marxist-Leninsts hold that it is beyond the power of the capitalist system to solve its ever-aggravating political and economic crises, still less to alter its fate of inevitable doom . . . It is our task as revolutionaries to accelerate its doom. Our policies and tactics may be altered, but our basic program of accomplishing the people's democratic revolution and proceeding to realize socialism and communism is unalterable. Likewise unalterable is the road of using the countryside to encircle the cities and seizing political power by armed force.

A similar statement, also publicized by Peking, was issued on the Fifth Anniversary of the Maoist Communist Party of the Philippines (December 26, 1973, Mao's birthday). It stressed that:

> There is no substitute for people's war . . . It is entirely correct for the armed units of the people's revolution to launch tactical offensives in the countryside at the enemy's weakest points within the context of a strategic defensive and for the underground in the cities and towns to bide its time, accumulate its strength, and generate revolutionary propaganda . . . Revolution is the main trend in the world today. The two superpowers, whether in contention or collusion with each other, are being isolated and given death-blows by countries wanting independence, nations wanting liberation, and the people wanting revolution.

Like similar material from other Peking-oriented Communist Parties, this document transmits more or less *en clair* the guidance given in less explicit form by such Peking organs as *Red Flag* and *People's Daily*. The evidence of guerrilla activities indicates that these exegeses of Mao Tse-tung's "proletarian revolutionary diplomatic line" are not mere "rhetoric," but must be taken seriously. Another exposition of Peking's strategy, in the American Maoist weekly *Guardian*, explained clearly the basis of the temporary deal with Nixon which facilitated the dual approach to America's allies or "puppets."

> The Chinese Communist Party has repeatedly emphasized that just because a government has joined in the struggle against the superpowers to one extent or another, the revolutionary forces in these countries must not give up their struggle. National and class struggles must continue even though particular governments may establish friendly relations with China. In fact, constantly developing the progressive forces within each country is a most necessary ingredient in building the front [that is, the united front led by China, ostensibly against superpower hegemony].

The *Guardian* goes on to explain:

> . . . reducing the power of both the USSR and USA will lead toward important struggles against neocolonialism and comprador bourgeois control . . . the struggle for national liberation (from colonial and neocolonial, feudal and semifeudal, comprador and big-bourgeoisie control) would be enhanced in a country free or mostly free of foreign control and thus of manipulation and support of the ruling group in power. And struggles for independence and then liberation often lead to revolution.

This is what is meant by the Chinese by their slogan, "Countries want independence, nations want liberation, and people want revolution."

Reports from the Subcontinent during 1973-74 indicated renewed Chinese assistance to Naxalite and other such extremist elements in India, Bangladesh, and Nepal, as well as conventional military aid to Pakistan. Some of these elements, notably the Mazumdar group of Naxalites, continued to defend Lin Piao's guerrilla line long after Peking muted its public support for extremism after Kissinger's visit to Peking and Lin's death. *Deshabrati*, the group's clandestine organ, has set 1975 as the target date for the "liberation" of India by armed force.

Reports from Burma and Thailand, as well as from Malaysia and the Philippines, also indicate an increase of insurgent activity, with detailed evidence of active support from China in the case of Burma. The problem arises, to what extent does such Chinese support of local insurgents represent the policy of the Peking regime? To what extent is it the result of inner-party struggles in Peking, or the insubordination of local commanders? The tactic of provoking trouble with foreign powers in the hope of embarrassing the central government is a familiar one in Chinese history, and was used during the Cultural Revolution. It could be used again in order to make difficulties for the civilianized element in the leadership, thought to be headed by Chou En-lai, and subjected to mounting criticism from a radical faction in the Communist Party during 1974.

In effect, the question is academic. This is because the two sets of activities—overt and covert, peaceful and violent—complement each other. A single issue of the Rangoon *Working People's Daily* (March 26, 1974) reported the opening of a bridge across the Salween River with Chinese aid, and the driving back of "foreign-assisted insurgents" in the Northeast; the accompanying map made it clear that they were Burma Communist Party guerrillas who have established themselves on the Shan Plateau in Kokang and Wa states bordering China since being thrown out of their original strongholds nearer Rangoon. In 1973, they pushed toward the Shan state of Kengtung, and occupied three towns in an attempt to set up a "liberated zone." A glance at the map will show that Kengtung city lies on the road from Kunming in southwest China across the Salween to Taunggyi and the central Mandalay-Rangoon railway, the spinal cord of Burma. The coordination of Chinese roadbuilding and other engineering projects abroad with insurgencies is a subject that deserves a monograph to itself: apart from the most obvious examples in Laos, Burma, and Nepal, cases may be found as far afield as Sudan and Central Africa. After the Army drove out the insurgents in December 1973, it was learned that they had included Chinese gunners and wireless operators. In Mongyang, one of the captured towns, Maoist slogans were found on the walls.

The Soviet journal *New Times* suggested (January 1974) that the BCP offensive was timed to influence the referendum on Burma's new constitution in December. A report adopted at an extraordinary congress of the ruling Burma Socialist Program Party in April 1974 blamed the agricultural producer cooperatives for rice shortages and curtailed their monopoly powers. Private traders were to be allowed to deal in grain as well as manufactured goods previously reserved for "people's" shops and cooperatives. The October congress purged left-wingers from the party, commended profit as a measure of success, and called for material incentives. In other words, the country was at last moving away from post-office socialism in a trend which is also to be noted in Delhi, Khartoum, and elsewhere. Consistent with this internal change is the modification of Burma's previous closed-door policy toward foreign participation in the development of its national resources. Apart from inviting foreign firms to prospect for offshore oil, Rangoon has joined the Asian Development Bank and signed agreements with it and the World Bank. President Ne Win made a tour of countries in the region in mid-1974, including Australia and Indonesia. It is to be hoped that the change of heart did not come too late to do Burma any good, given the deteriorating international climate for finance and aid. The country remains a potential window onto the Indian Ocean for southwest China.

Whether or not the project for a canal and/or pipeline across the Kra Isthmus comes to fruition, the security of Thailand and West Malaysia is of direct concern to Japan and other countries trading across the Indian Ocean. Here again, the policies of the PRC and of the Democratic Republic of Vietnam (Hanoi) are not encouraging. With propaganda support from China, the Communist Party of Thailand tried to exploit the events of October 1973 in Bangkok, with which it had little to do initially. The Peking *People's Daily* attacked the new government of Sanya Dharmasakdi a few days after it took power, declaring that "the just demands of the students and people had not been realised," and that neither armed repression nor "deceitful tricks" could stop the advance of the student movement and the people's struggle. Voice of the People of Thailand broadcasts spelled out the message even more clearly, calling on the students to complete the overthrow of "imperialism, feudalism, and bureaucrat capitalism" by coordinating their struggle with the armed struggle of the guerrillas in the countryside. According to a Thai Government White Paper of 1972, Chinese troops of Meo ethnic origin had been sent into northern Thailand to help tribal insurgents, access having been improved by the Chinese-built road through northern Laos which stops at Pak Beng, about 20 miles from the Thai border. A defector revealed in 1973 that the Pathet Lao had begun to return 3,000 guerrillas of Lao Thai origin to Thailand after training at Dong Ha in North Vietnam, to build up a liberated area next to Laos, where they were no longer needed.

In spite of continuing Chinese support for the insurgents, the Thai government moved from the semiofficial contacts of 1972-73, under cover of sporting exchanges, to visits by senior officials in 1974. The Deputy Foreign Minister, Major General Chartichai Chunhawan, led a group from the Ministry of Commerce to China in January, and got 50,000 tons of oil at a "friendship" price. Air Chief Marshal Dawee went in February as Chairman of the Olympic Committee, and said on his return that Chou En-lai had told him that China no longer supported the insurgents since Thailand now had a democratic government. But the value of such assurances is hard to judge. On April 10, the Voice of the People of Thailand again called on the Thai people to overthrow the government.

Against this background, and in view of the continuing fighting in Indochina and the Muslim rebellion in the Philippines, the prospects of ASEAN achieving its goals of neutralization and national resilience appeared as remote as ever in 1974, although meetings of Foreign Ministers and other senior officials mooted proposals for a constitution and a nonaggression pact between the member countries. In May, the Foreign Ministers, meeting in Jakarta, agreed that their views on security would not carry much weight in the world until they also wield economic power—that is, by economic cooperation and by forming a sort of cartel for raw materials, including oil, timber, tin, copper, rubber, natural gas, and agricultural products. It was also decided to set up a permanent secretariat in Jakarta as ASEAN headquarters.

The general idea of forming a producers cartel is not too far from ideas now strongly pushed by Peking for its own purposes. The notion of reinsurance with Peking for fear of Hanoi, which some deride as the "norodomino theory" in view of its application by

Prince Norodom Sihanouk, is in effect anti-Soviet. Fear of Peking and of the local Overseas Chinese automatically implies opposition to the continued Balkanization of Indochina required by Peking's policy, and raises the possibility of a Southeast Asian "collective security" arrangement with more or less Soviet backing.

6

Interests of Australia and Japan

There are two "developed" societies which are very closely concerned with the stability and security of the Indian Ocean though actually located in the Western Pacific—Japan and Australia.

As is well known, the bulk of Australia's population and resources, and the national capital, are tucked away in one green corner of the vast and desert continent. Western Australia, which produces much of its newly-found mineral wealth, might as well be a separate island for practical purposes, including defense. Port Hedland is about the same distance from the naval base at Sydney as it is from Shanghai or Nagasaki. According to an article in the *Journal of the Australian Institute of International Affairs*, significantly entitled, "Are Western Australians Worth Defending?", it would probably take almost three months to move a fully equipped division from eastern Australia to the west—that is, if any attempt were to be made by the eastern states to defend the west against a threat from the Indian Ocean.

For historical reasons, an ostrich-like attitude on defense matters and the international environment generally has gained wide acceptance in Australia, so that Coral Bell, a leading Australian writer on strategy and world affairs, could write (even before the Whitlam Labor Government took power):

> No other country of the Western tradition is more vulnerable than Australia to any international storms that may arise in the Indian Ocean, and none has a clearer or more direct interest in the construction, if possible, of a viable security system cover-

ing that very extensive portion of the globe. Yet it could hardly be maintained that this viewpoint has had much visible influence on Australian public opinion until very recent times.

Under the Australian Labor Party, this situation has become considerably worse. In reaction to the Liberal Party's ploy of arousing and exploiting fears of foreign, especially Communist, "threats" to entrench itself in power for a quarter of a century, Labor has promoted a new orthodoxy to the effect that no "threat" could materialize for ten to 15 years, and that armed forces were in any case an "archaic" survival in the modern world. Those on the left wing showed a marked predilection for realignment of Australia's trade and diplomacy towards the Communist (especially Asian Communist) bloc, and even the Prime Minister tried to project the image of an "independent" foreign policy while eschewing its prerequisite—indigenous military strength.

As King Frederick of Prussia used to say, "politics without armaments is like music without instruments." But one road to power—or at least publicity—for the powerless has always been to pose as champion or unifier of the many and weak against the strong and few. The pan-Africanism of Nkrumah, the Arabism of Gamal Abdel Nasser, even de Gaulle's Third World policy illustrate this cardinal precept, not to mention Soviet postwar efforts to mobilize "peace forces" and Afro-Asian allies, first in lieu of, then in support of, their own nuclear weapons.

Given the power logic of the Pacific, and thanks to a particular concatenation of domestic and international events, a special toothless variety of nationalism, self-assertion, and "world-role seeking" was bound to emerge in Australia, Canada, some Latin American countries, and Japan. It was bound to take the form of asserting "independence"—of the United States, who else? And the most obvious and domestically advantageous way was to do obeisance to Peking.

In both Australia and Japan, the "China issue" has long been involved with domestic politics and security policy. Japan's security depended on the agreement with the United States, and hence (by a series of other commitments) on support for the Republic of China on Taiwan. Successive Australian governments also felt obliged publicly to signal loyalty to Washington, the "great and powerful friend," by supporting its controversial attitude to Peking, though representations were made in private in favor of a change. Public opinion on the "China question" in Japan, manipulated by opportunist Japanese business and political interests and latterly by Peking's own apparatus of "people's diplomacy," and also by the Taiwan lobby, reached a point where objective discussion of the real China across the water was hardly possible or even relevant. "China" had become a shibboleth to define sets of attitudes and emotions about Japan's internal politics, "progressive" or "reactionary."

Precisely because Australia lacked the close historical ties and cultural similarities which Japan has with China, it was even easier for China to become a "free-floating symbol" in Australian public opinion—as one Australian academic put it after carrying out a survey. Since almost nobody in the country had more than the haziest ideas about the real China, it was easy for the opposition Labor Party and its supporters in the media to denounce the Canberra government's policy of recognizing Taipei as an example of foolish subservience to Washington. Against the traditional bogey of Red hordes dripping down the map, public opinion was presented with an equally distorted picture of an "amazingly docile" China, whose main aim in life was to improve social services and cure more people by acupuncture.

Undoubtedly, Mr. Whitlam's well-publicized visit to Peking before the 1972 elections greatly contributed to his success. In Japan, Prime Minister Sato's reluctance to ditch Taiwan for Peking hastened his downfall. What obviously threw both the Japanese and Australian governments into disarray was Kissinger's secret visit to Peking— contemporaneous with Whitlam's, though he was not told about it either. So it came about that Pierre Elliott Trudeau, Gough Whitlam, Kakuei Tanaka, and the rest were not "doing a de Gaulle" after all in going to Peking; they were only "doing a Nixon." But the significance of the same act done by them and by the leader of one of the superpowers was completely different.

As far as the stability of the western Pacific is concerned, the effect of the "Nixon shocks" (first, the China switch, second, the economic measures against Japan) was to alienate Japanese public opinion and political leadership from the United States, and impose an agonising reappraisal of Japan's role in world politics, which will take a long time to work itself out. One of the probable results is a reorientation and diversification of Japan's trade, which will increase the importance for Japan of access to the Indian Ocean area, its approaches, and especially to Indonesia and Australia. Soon after Dr. Kissinger's first visit to Peking, realization dawned in Tokyo that the security treaty was no longer an instrument for using Japan and Okinawa to "contain" China, but rather a means of "policing" Japan, which had become an economic threat to its erstwhile protector, and encouraging it to do business with China and Siberia, as well as to pick up some former US responsibilites in the Pacific under the Guam Doctrine.

In Canberra, Liberal politicians and government officials privately expressed puzzlement and dismay, but the security implications of the new alignments in the Pacific at first failed to engage the attention of public opinion. The snap election of 1974 did stimulate a public debate in which the role of ANZUS and US communications facilities in Australia were questioned. Some arguments were put forward by senior naval officers, defense officials, and others calling for more attention to the defense of Western Australia, and for forces capable of operating in the Indian Ocean. Even if a decision were to be taken in 1974 to acquire such naval and air forces and/or to "go nuclear," which is exceedingly unlikely, Australia's military weakness during the necessary lead time of eight years or so would be quite disproportionate to its resources and strategic importance. In any case, a Labor government would tend to go on playing the present double game of voting and running with the Third World hares (to the exasperation of America), while still relying on the sea-hounds of the Seventh Fleet for security.

In the *Canberra Times* of June 19, 1973, the former head of the Australian diplomatic service, Sir Alan Watt, pointed out that Australia had voted for a UN resolution requiring independence for 17 small territories, including the Cocos Islands in the Indian Ocean, which are administered by Australia. The question was asked in Parliament, Since Australia had voted for the resolution, when were the Cocos Islands going to be made independent? Mr. Whitlam replied that "if a resolution is 90 percent acceptable, one votes for it; it does not mean that one votes for every individual aspect of it." He added that no consideration had been given to independence for these islands and he did not think anyone seriously believed that independence would be appropriate. The other territories in question were American Samoa, the Bahamas, Bermuda, British Virgin Islands, Brunei, Cayman Islands, Gilbert and Ellice Islands, Guam, Montserrat, New Hebrides, Pitcairn, St. Helena, Seychelles, Solomon Islands, Turks and Caicos Islands and the US Virgin Islands. In view of the strategic importance of several of these places, it is hardly credible that any statesman should imagine that *independence* was the point of the UN Assembly resolution, or that its practicability was a consideration of interest to those who framed it. The purpose was evidently to make trouble for Western countries and promote anticolonialist feeling among Third World countries, facing the former with the choice of voting against their own and their allies' interests or else antagonizing the Afro-Asians.

Voting for such resolutions without the slightest intention that they should be put into effect may eventually boomerang against the Labor government, especially if in practice it maintains its defense links with America. Or else it might follow the clearly-expressed inclinations of the increasingly powerful left wing and cut the US painter altogether. In the first case, Australia would continue to be praised in public and despised in private by the Indian Ocean politicians— who, after all, have not led such a sheltered life. In the second case, the lunatic fringe of Australian politics sees close ties with China as a reinsurance against domination and exploitation by American and Japanese "monopoly capital;" while non-Australian optimists suggest scenarios such as the "Pacific maritime triangle"—Australia, Japan, and Indonesia—espoused by Professor Z. Brzezinski, or the development of ASEAN. But it is hard to see how any of these arrangements could work without the benevolent interest of the United States. Either way, Australia could exert little influence over events in its environment; and however much its spokesmen may denounce racism in South Africa, it will always be discriminated against and isolated as an allegedly "racist" country in the end.

Thus, from the point of view of Indian Ocean politics, the present Australia is not so much an actor as an arena in which outside powers will contend for access and influence, and which the United States, Japan, China, and the USSR in particular will seek to use as a stepping stone or, as Chou En-lai put it, a "gateway to the south." Apart from its small population and enormous coastline, the real reason for this passivity lies in the uninformed apathy of public opinion about foreign affairs, which is largely due to the "tyranny of distance" and the uncertainty among the elite as to goals and roles in the new world situation. (It was not for nothing that the Australian Institute of International Affairs held its 1974 Conference under the title, "Advance Australia Where?")

Japan, on the other hand, is an important actor in Indian Ocean politics, although equally uncertain about where exactly its overall policy is headed. Its enormous economic interests are bound to increase its political involvement in the area, and could conceivably lead to a military role in some form, depending on which option Tokyo finds itself stuck with out of those left open by President Nixon's international plumbers. To put it crudely, the combination of political and economic rebuffs from America increased existing pressures for Japan to seek its markets and sources of raw materials elsewhere, especially nearby in Siberia and China, with the ultimate likely result that its society and government could "go Communist" or return to militarism—precisely what Dr. Kissinger reportedly wished to avoid.

Even before the "shocks," more than 40 percent of Japanese imports (by purchase value) came from or through the Indian Ocean area, about half of this total coming from Europe. In 1969, Japan was dependent on imports for 99.8 percent of its oil, 85 percent of its iron ore, and 72 percent of its copper. Even for those raw materials traditionally produced at home, the tendency was toward greater reliance on imports. Japan's volume of consumption of raw materials is second only to the United States, and is constantly rising. With the post-shock reduction of exports to the United States, which used to be about 30 percent, more exports, too, have been carried across the Indian Ocean.

Before the energy crisis, 30 Japanese oil tankers of over 200,000 tons each were passing through the Malacca Strait eight or nine times a year, carrying about 90 percent of Japan's oil requirements from the Persian Gulf (most of the rest being from Indonesia—some 70 percent of that country's production). The importance of the Malacca Strait has already been touched on. The three littoral states have reportedly considered banning the passage of ships of more than 200,000 tons. In that case, Japan would lose about Y10,000 million, or $315 million, per year. If 30 supertankers had to be diverted to the Lombok-Makassar Straits, loss per ship would be about Y5 million per day, representing four days extra on the journey (7660 miles to the Gulf instead of 6,500), and resulting in a price hike of Y30 per kilolitre of oil. A supertanker such as the 350,000-ton Nisseki Maru already takes the Lombok-Makassar route full, but returns via the Malacca Strait.

Before the crisis, Japan was importing 200 million tons of Middle East crude per annum, carried in a fleet of 220 tankers averaging 90,000 tons, and each making about ten trips a year. If the Malacca and other straits should be closed to them by political sanctions, insurgent hijacking, or other easily conceivable means, Japan would be very vulnerable to blackmail—as Tokyo proved itself to be during the 1973 energy crisis.

Forgetting, perhaps, the reasons for Pearl Harbor, Defense Secretary Melvin Laird said on March 19, 1972, that self-interest would require Japan to establish a naval presence in the Indian Ocean. The Director General of the Japanese Defense Agency, Masumi Esaki, stated a month later that it was "inconceivable that Maritime Self-Defense Force craft could ever operate in the Strait of Malacca, let alone the Indian Ocean." Nevertheless, Japan's growing political and economic crisis, as well as the increasingly difficult Pacific environment, suggest the strong possibility of an imposed self-reliance and return to nationalism, including the acquisition of nuclear missile submarines as a deterrent. The alternatives would be:

1. To try and stay hitched to America. A wide spectrum of Japanese opinion has expressed profound disillusion and distrust *vis-à-vis* the United States. Such a policy would be suicidal for the politicians of the Liberal Democratic Party.

2. To identify closely with China or the Soviet Union. Though Tanaka rode high at first on his pro-Peking policy, he was soon rated by the *Far Eastern Economic Review* (May 13, 1974) as perhaps the most unpopular leader in recent Japanese history. The complications that would be raised by identifying too completely with China (and drawing the fire of the increasingly influential pro-Soviet Japan Communist Party, the pro-Taiwan *Seirankai* group, and others), or with Russia—the hereditary enemy—would defeat any politician, whether "pure" like Tanaka or "bureaucratic" in the ordinary LDP tradition.

3. To try to form some quadrilateral trade, security, and non-aggression arrangements with the US, USSR, and China. Although this would be the most desirable outcome, these powers are more likely to try and pull Tokyo their way rather than agree to anchor Japan in the middle.

The deal concluded with the Soviets in June 1974 for the development of coal mines in Yakutia has opened the way for others which have been under discussion for years, including an oil and gas project involving a pipeline to Nakhodka—which, as Peking complains, could be used to supply the 1.3 million Soviet troops on China's frontier and the Soviet fleet operating from Vladivostok into the Indian Ocean. The Sino-Japanese aviation agreement signed on April 20, 1974, after surprising Chinese concessions, hardly compensates Peking for Japan's plunge into Siberia.

Because of Japanese media concern to keep correspondents in Peking, public opinion is fed mainly favorable reports on China. It is too easy to identify discontent with inflation, pollution, and similar problems with past pro-American governments, and to equate nationalism and self-assertion with being against America and "therefore" for Peking. The solution most likely to recommend itself to the divided and disoriented LDP government is to coopt the militant right-wing nationalist revival. In exactly the same way as some of the Indian planners around Mrs. Gandhi, the rightists calculate that the growth industries of future are those connected with defense and the development of ocean resources; that a military, naval, and nuclear build-up would give the people a tangible national goal and create ongoing *faits accomplis* in industry to justify the limitation of unrealistic Socialist measures on the ground of efficiency in defense of the realm.

Thus, direct Japanese involvement in the military/political balance of the Indian Ocean area cannot be ruled out. Economic involvement is already considerable, and is likely to continue growing—especially in Australia and Southeast Asia. Australia has special significance for Japan as a source of energy as well as minerals. Over 53 percent of all Australian minerals and metals exports are to Japan; and it is estimated that by 1979-80, these exports will be between A\$1,500 and A\$1,900 million. Australia is also expected to supply 40 percent of Japan's imports of coking coal in the future, and Japan hopes to import liquified natural gas from the Northwest Shelf area by 1978. But the most important possibility is a uranium enrichment plant, to be built in Australia with Japanese capital. The Australian government has already approved export licenses for sales of uranium oxide to Japan between 1975 and 1986. Under the Liberals, it also asked state governments to study possible locations for an enrichment plant.

Consideration of the involvement of the western Pacific nations in the Indian Ocean would be incomplete without reference to China. Mention has already been made to its involvements in Pakistan, Tanzania, and elsewhere, and the indirect approach via "liberation struggles" and related international agitation. At present, China's merchant marine and Navy are relatively puny, but considerable progress has been made. Several all-Chinese cargo vessels of 10,000 tons and tankers of 15,000 tons have been built. Articles in the official press have called for a naval build-up, and this has been put into effect with the construction of new missile ships and evidence of a program for Polaris-type nuclear submarines. The Peking *People's Daily* wrote on June 4 1970, that:

> Whether or not we vigorously strive to develop the shipbuilding industry and build a powerful navy as well as a powerful maritime fleet is an important issue concerning whether or not we want to consolidate our national defense, strengthen the dictatorship of the proletariat, liberate Taiwan and finally unify our motherland, develop the freight business, build socialism, and support world revolution.

7

Conclusions

What called world attention to the Indian Ocean "power vacuum" was the increase in visible Soviet naval activity from March 1968, closely following the then British government's ill-advised advertisement of its intention to withdraw from east of Suez. But this naval presence is not as important as the Russian economic, political, and military involvement in countries around the periphery, in such forms as great engineering and land communications projects and proxy use of local armed forces, as once practiced by the British Raj. Incidentally, the British presence in the area is still not inconsiderable, and could, with the French and other concerned powers (other than the superpowers), form the basis of a common approach to some aspects of security in the area in cooperation with the regional states. This would be a better formula than the attempt by some of these countries to try and exclude all outside forces in order to strive for oceanic supremacy themselves. This would inevitably draw in the superpowers even more. The Soviet Union's activities in the area are part of its global attempt to extend its influence and implement the foreign policy of a superpower. Competition with the People's Republic of China on many levels is an important part of this policy, and the Indian Ocean—containing much of the Third World—is a major theater of Sino-Soviet competition. Opening of the Suez Canal would transform the situation to the advantage of the USSR, though not as dramatically as is sometimes alleged.

The PRC has provided a few naval craft to Tanzania and Sri Lanka, but so far has competed for influence with the USSR in the area without "showing the flag" in the conventional manner, partly

75

because it has been more willing and able to exploit local "people's wars," while winning the confidence of certain governments with aid on very "soft" terms. This is the principle of walking on two legs, or, as the late Marshal Lin Piao put it, "the locomotive of revolution runs on two rails." Japan has won economic influence, and is involved in schemes for improving communications in Africa, for example, which superficially resemble those of China. But, Japan has generally been identified with conservative rather than insurgent forces in the continent, and has no card in hand equivalent to China's links with "liberation" groups. This exposes Japan to pressure—for example, over the fact that Rhodesian shops are full of Japanese goods. Pilloried in the United Nations as a "notorious sanctions breaker," Japan annouced in June 1974 that it would not give visas to South Africans visiting for sports, educational, and cultural exchanges. This action, taken in obedience to a UN resolution, opens the way to cutting other links with South Africa and other markets and sources of supply. It is expected that some of Japan's raw materials requirements will increase by 300 percent in the coming decade. As is well known, some 90 percent of its oil requirements come from the Middle East; and essentials such as copper and zinc also cross the Indian Ocean from Africa. Japan's diversification policy has tended to reduce direct dependence on Asia for imports and exports; but it has also caused many countries, notably Indonesia and Australia, to depend more on Japan as a major market. By 1980, Japan's share of Asian trade is expected to rise to 49 percent, but the importance of Asian trade for Japan is decreasing. For example, Japan imports 50 percent of its demand for bauxite from Australia, but this represents 80 percent of Australia's bauxite exports. Some 90 percent of Indonesian nickel, 85 percent of its timber, 100 percent of iron dust, and between 87 and 90 percent of oil go to Japan. But this oil does not amount to ten percent of total imports by Japan.

This imbalance threatens to distort the economic and political structures of the smaller Asian-Pacific countries, whether they allow "growth without development" to generate social unrest and give excessive power to foreign firms, or set up centralizing institutions to deal with the problem; for these, too, are likely to acquire excessive or unconstitutional powers to mould the domestic economy and society as required by external forces.

United States interest in the area derives primarily from its importance to Europe and Japan. The energy crisis has added to this interest. In view of the special relationship established between the US and Saudi Arabia in 1974 to meet the former's astronomical oil needs, the American interest in the "stability" of the Indian Ocean area must increase.

But what is "stability," and what are the threats to it? What is usually meant by stability is safe conditions for trade—not political and social stagnation, which in the end endanger them. The dangers in the area are not so much due to direct great power interference, but the other way round. War on their scale has become too destructive, and more important, too expensive even to prepare, so that politicians on each side may regard each other (as Khrushchev's memoirs suggest) as allies in the fight to cut down the budget demands of the military.

If the big powers are too strong to fight, the small ones are—by their very weakness, lack of cohesion, and Balkanization—likely to be the cause or scene of all kinds of "destabilizing" violence, ranging from delinquency, organized crime, piracy (with or without political cover), riots, guerrilla warfare, and full-scale replays of World War II tank battles and air raids.

When it dawns on governmental committees and similar bodies that the military response is the easy—but wrong—way out, the conclusion may all too often be that what tons of bombs cannot do, tons of PL480 wheat or "massive aid" will do in order to hasten "growth" and "development." The next stage of sophistication is reached when experience shows that such aid, and modernization in general, is profoundly "destabilizing," and in fact has been responsible for much of the unrest in the postwar era that is so often blamed on Communist subversion or neocolonialist oppression, according to standpoint.

A school of thought has now emerged in the United States and other "developed" countries which is aware of "the threat from the Third World." A perceptive article in *Foreign Policy* (Summer 1973) points out that insofar as any common pattern may be discerned in the heterogeneous "Third World," the priority for its elites will be "economic and social development." But such development involves four requirements which are irreconcilable; the article lists them without pointing this out:

1. "Desire for economic social progress is . . . increasingly likely to dominate internal politics."

2. The less developed countries (LDCs) learned that "growth alone" cannot guarantee the politically central objectives of economic policy—"full employment, relatively stable prices, equitable income distribution, and ultimately an enhanced quality of life." In spite of "growth," unemployment exceeds 20 percent in many LDC's, there are 100 million more illiterates then 20 years ago, and two thirds of the children suffer from malnutrition.

3. The LDCs will increasingly reject dictation from outsiders of all types: foreign governments, international agencies, multinational corporations. This is partly due to the shortcomings they perceive in "aid" and models of "development" offered by these outsiders, and partly due to nationalist desires to overcome the feeling of dependence on the rich.

4. "The Third World will continue to need outside help. Few LDCs will be able to meet their economic and social needs without steady infusions of foreign exchange."

The article goes on to point out that the Third World retains some importance for US security, but its major impact is economic. Much of this impact relates to the position of the United States in its triangular economic relationship with Europe and Japan.

> The pervasive and growing economic interpenetration among these three industrialized areas is increasingly important to the welfare of other key groups. Severe political tensions thus arise. The foreign economic policies of each area are increasingly politicized and increasingly polarized and have become potentially explosive.

This economic interpenetration also extends to the Third World, as a result of which the US stake in the Third World is growing, and the leverage of the Third World to affect the United States is growing. Leverage could be exerted through withholding supplies to one or more of the industrialized countries, discriminatory price rises (for example, against the US and in favor of Europe and Japan), selective use of export earnings from oil and other raw materials, confiscation of or other action against foreign investments, repudiation of debts, price-cutting of manufactured exports, expansion of competitive exports by becoming "pollution havens," and so forth. Neither gunboat nor dollar diplomacy will suffice to deal with these forms of attacks, which have all been tried out already and are likely to be used by LDC governments in future even if they know the results will be against their true "national interest." Domestic political pressures to use them will prove too strong. The LDCs may increase their leverage by playing on disputes among the US, Europe, and Japan; in the absence of overriding Cold War unity, these powers may engage in "bitter" competition for Third World support.

This American scenario is quoted at length because it is extraordinarily similar to that propounded by Peking, allowing for differences of jargon and underlying assumptions. What is surprising is that this and similar Western analyses go on to argue that since the "threat" is primarily economic, it can be dealt with by economic measures such as liberalization of trade and more aid, reform of the international monetary system, organizations of consumer states to match producer cartels like OPEC, and thrusting the LDCs into positions of international responsibility so as to make them act "responsibly."

Such measures are doubtless desirable. But the underlying assumption is that the LDCs must and can "develop"—that is to say, reach something like the life-style of America, Europe, and Japan. It is, however, very doubtful if the actual resources for such "development" can be found, whatever financial arrangements may be worked out. Moreover, there is increasing resistance on the part of donor countries to soaring demands for aid. Theo Sommer, Editor of *Die Zeit*, remarked in *Newsweek* (January 21, 1974) that the Third

World "looks like a bottomless pit." It is much more likely that a combination of the pressures from disillusioned public opinion in the LDCs and from Chinese and similar anti-Western propaganda will lead to escalating confrontations in which the United Nations and other international organizations, conferences, and similar forums will be used by the poor countries to divide and put pressure on the "rich."

What divides rich and poor individuals in the LDCs is essentially status rather than levels of consumption of material goods. The appeal of Mao's regime in China is to the idea of an egalitarianism imposed at a low level of consumption by an elite which is interested in power, not ostentatious wealth. Peking's claim to mobilize and lead the Third World is justified by exactly the same pose as protector of the poor and *primus inter pares,* "never seeking hegemony." If the governments of the Indian Ocean countries continue to attempt the impossible, the appeal of Peking's revolutionary doctrines must increase in the long run.

In the short term, the attempt to fulfill Afro-Asian expectations of an Americanized (or Sovietized) life-style is already taxing existing political and economic structures in the LDCs, and planners are becoming aware of the dangers. For example, Indonesia's Center for Strategic and International Studies is already considering how the *internationalization of production* (investment by multinationals, and so forth) can be made to bring about the *internationalization of consumption* (raising level in LDCs). Faced with the polarizing and transforming influence of Japanese capital and technology, they naturally propose setting up a "power entity on a national scale which can serve as a countervailing power against both multinational corporations and foreign national enterprises." This entity might, in effect, constitute a local branch of the emerging global power elite of cosmopolitan businessmen, international technocrats, and members of professional associations. It would tend to bypass, or even manipulate and substitute for, the established structures and constitutional government (as is alleged to occur with "Japan, Inc."), and might therefore fall into the wrong hands and become a "state within the state," favoring a polarization towards authoritarianism and elite nationalism, on the one hand, and populist agitation against what would be called bureaucratic capital, the comprador bourgeoisie, or "imitation foreign devils" on the other.

The "development" process logically involves an internationalization of values and life-style as well as of consumption, which is also neither completely feasible nor desirable. The experience of Sri Lanka, the Malagasy Republic, and many of the other countries of the Indian Ocean area shows that apart from the well-known effects of the population explosion and the failure of economic growth to keep up with it, a major source of unrest is the maladaptation and excessive cost of Western-style educational systems and the impossibility of finding jobs for graduates of the system once they have got through it. Experiments are being made in Indonesia with new methods of village education, and ways of developing a new life-style, which will provide status and satisfaction without depending on Western-level symbols and consumption. In the end, such indigenous initiatives may prove to be more important for the stability of the area than any made by outside powers. On the state level, too, means must be found to give status, and appease the "nationalism" which arises from lack of it, without the costly and dangerous gadgetry which nations perceive to be necessary. Meanwhile, on the level of what governments can in practice deal with, the multiplicity of relations in the "mandala pattern" which is emerging from the end of bipolarity is going to make it increasingly difficult for chancelleries, trade departments, and other agencies of government to follow what is going on, and far more to make informed decisions about problems across the multicentered and centrifugal world.

Australian Attitudes

Since this essay has been written in Australia, it seems pertinent to conclude with some further remarks on Australian attitudes to the security of the Indian Ocean and of Australian territory.

The original conception of this study excluded developed countries of the Southern Hemisphere—Australia and South Africa—because of their presumed stability and their military and economic strength.

South Africa was briefly mentioned because of the race and guerrilla issue, and the increasing acceptance by world public opinion that it is worse for Africans to be bossed by white racists than butchered by black tribalists. The accession to power of Labor governments in Australia and New Zealand in 1972, and the decision of the former to reduce defense forces, on the assumption that there will be no "threat" to the country for 15 years or so, changed the situation in the eastern part of the Southern Hemisphere to a considerable extent. From the Chinese point of view, as Chou En-lai has remarked, Australia is the "gateway to the south"—that is to say, to the Indian Ocean via Southeast Asia.

The strategic assessment that no specific "threat" to Australia could now be forecast was reached against the general background of what is commonly seen as the "detente" in international relations, or the end of the Cold War. A number of Defense Department officials and officers have publicly dissociated themselves from this assessment, including the former Chief of Naval Staff, Vice Admiral Sir R. Peek. Brigadier J. G. Hooton, a former Director of Defense, resigned in April 1974 in protest against neglect of defense preparedness and has also spoken out on the matter. Officials remaining in the Department allege that owing to the politicization of the public service, Defense and Foreign Affairs position papers are self-censored so as to fit the preconceptions and purposes of their political masters.

The attitude of the Liberal and Labor Parties has differed only in degree, both accepting literally the "no threat" misconception. In fact, Defense and Intelligence officials point out privately that predictions about the international environment and emerging threats can only be made for two or three years ahead, whereas the lead time for developing adequate defenses is eight to ten years. It is also interesting to note that Peking vociferously rejects the notion that SALT, the Nixon pilgrimages, and so forth, imply a detente. On the contrary, it warns that in the present situation of multipolar imbalance, the Soviets are more dangerous than ever. Peking advises non-Communist countries (both in public and in private) to keep up and expand their defense capability.

Can the Chinese have a point? On logical grounds, it seems unjustified to reason that since the future is so unpredictable, "she'll be right". No *easily identifiable* threat does not imply no threat. On practical grounds, it is becoming obvious that what is meant by detente in Europe means the final ratification of Soviet neocolonial control in Eastern Europe. What is meant by detente in Asia is, similarly, confirmation of China's claim to Taiwan and ratification of other Communist gains which hitherto always seemed to them threatened and temporary (Korea and Indochina). The West is brought in (in the form of US troops in Taiwan, American and Japanese investment, trade with and investment from Europe) to shore up an essentially shaky Chinese government whose internal position, after the Cultural Revolution and Marshal Lin Piao's attempts to assassinate Chairman Mao, is parlous. For the first time since 1949, the official *People's Daily* in March 1973 reported people keeping "accounts" in anticipation of a change of regime, in order to take revenge when it comes.

The uneasy tripartite balance between the factions of Chou En-lai and Madame Mao, and combinations of the military, is reminiscent of the situation in the last days of the Roman Republic, except that for the parallel to be nearer, Octavian should have drowned on the way to Parthia after three bungled attempts to kill Julius Caesar. Since the Sino-American Shanghai communique, US forces in Taiwan are in a sense working for Mao, preventing any Unilateral Declaration of Independence by Taiwan under Japanese economic and Soviet political aegis. The purpose of US policy seems similar to that of the powers after the Boxer Rebellion of 1900—to prop up a weak Chinese government against Russia, precisely mirroring Peking's policy of supporting the declining imperialist force against the rising threat of "social-imperialist" Russia.

Precisely because the simplistic bipolar alignments of the Cold War are no more, it is impossible to predict for so far as 15 or 20 years ahead what will happen in the extremely volatile areas covered in this study, especially in the Persian Gulf, the Indian Subcontinent, and both continental and maritime Southeast Asia. The Soviet and Chinese planning staffs, especially naval staffs, cannot but anticipate that their opposite numbers will pursue a forward policy. By the well-known mechanism of self-fulfilling prophecy, each will interpret moves made to forestall the other as evidence of the need to make more moves to "get in there before they do." It is significant that Peking Radio's English language service to Australia frequently quotes at length such material as Lord Carrington's statement that the Soviet Union continues to increase its forces on a scale far surpassing the reasonable requirements of self-defense, and Lord Chalfont's article in the *Times* (June 15, 1973) warning against the belief that the Soviet military threat had disappeared. Both warned against any relaxation in NATO's defense program. The welcome given to Mr. Heath in Peking in May 1974 was also entirely intended to strengthen EEC and NATO.

As President Nyerere of Tanzania has astutely remarked, the situation is shaping up like that obtaining when the European powers relaxed tensions between themselves at the Berlin Conference of 1884-85. The British and French, and others, scrambled for Africa and other colonies to get in first. Then they shared things out amicably—but it did not greatly comfort the Africans. In the same way, the Soviets offer to protect small and middle powers against alleged Chinese expansionism with collective security treaties, and the Chinese offer to mobilize small and middle powers to resist hegemony by the superpowers, especially Russia. This process is likely to end up, in conjunction with the activities of Japan, Europe, and the US striving for resources and markets, in a situation most detrimental to the independence and security of the small and middle powers.

In concrete terms, Sino-Soviet rivalry over the Indonesian archipelago and the Indochinese peninsula (in the old-fashioned sense, including Burma and Thailand) will take advantage of any faltering in Indonesia's progress to try and line up that country. Given the delicate position of the Overseas Chinese in internal affairs, Jakarta may either follow Kuala Lumpur in trying to fix things with Peking over their heads, or else move toward the remoter and apparently safer Soviet Union. In that case, it is not inconceivable that in a very short space of time, a treaty relationship similar to that between the USSR and India, Iraq, and Egypt would bring modern, properly maintained and manned Soviet warships and aircraft to Australia's doorstep. Even a slight acquaintance with the outlook of Soviet decisionmakers, as revealed for example in Khrushchev's memoirs, would suggest that they could not fail to take advantage of such a situation if Australia allows its defense forces to run down—especially if the argument of "revolutionary defeatism" was being raised in the country. This is the argument that it is futile to arm at all, because no Australian forces would be strong enough to defeat a superpower. The point is not in any imaginary eventual invasion, but in the political climate created by a feeling of powerlessness which would make it possible, indeed inevitable, for an outside armed entity (not necessarily a state, but even pirates, terrorists, or what not) to dictate terms without even needing to employ violence.

The notions are sometimes expressed in Australia—even in academic and official circles—that the use of military force in international affairs is somehow "archaic," that there are no more colonies in the world except those of France and Portugal, that the Cold War is "over," and that talk about communism is "garbage." All this reveals an extraordinary confusion of mind. Old-fashioned talk about monolithic "international communism" is garbage, to be sure. But Soviet spying, subversion, and naval expansion, and Chinese measures to counter them are not. Military force is being used daily to cow peoples under occupation, and to try and overthrow the incumbent authorities in Eastern Europe, Palestine, and other parts of the Middle East, and also in many parts of Asia and Africa, not to mention urban guerrilla warfare in Latin America and Ireland. The outlying domains of the Tsar and the Manchu Emperor, now incorporated into the USSR and the PRC, are just as much colonies as—for example—Angola and Mozambique have been, and even more colonial than South Africa and Rhodesia, which are no longer ruled from the former metropolis. In his speeches to arouse the Athenians against Philip of Macedon, Demosthenes insisted that it was no use speculating whether he was sick or dead. The way they went on neglecting their defenses, they would raise up another Philip to overwhelm them. Indeed, they got Alexander. Today, to confuse no specific threat with no threat at all is a sure way to create one.

A Chinese state or interest group may in the future become a danger to Australia, if only to exclude other influences (such as India, Indonesia, Japan, and Russia) from this rich and underpopulated

continent. The revelations about Lin Piao's plotting made at the
Peking Party Congress of August 1973, and during the bizarre cam-
paign to "criticize Confucius and Lin Piao" which raged during 1974,
perhaps should not be taken literally. But the veiled attacks on per-
sons still in power suggest that anything may happen at any time in
China.

An article published in the *Peking Review* of April 26, 1974, for
example, discussed how in ancient times a certain Fan Sui opposed
the concept of a ruler sharing power with the feudal lords, and advanced that of establishing a single centralized state. On the question
of wiping out the independent states, he reversed the former policy
of "attacking the distant states and keeping friendly relations with
nearby states," and was appointed Prime Minister by the ruler of
Ch'in, the state which eventually unified and gave its name to China.
But he was "sitting on a volcano" because of the influence of the
former feudal lords. Hence, he "wavered and asked to return the seal
of Prime Minister because of illness." Chinese and Sinologist readers
of this sort of material could not fail to see the analogies with Premier
Chou En-lai, who had failed to turn up to important functions "because of illness," and was clearly in political difficulties after the re-
shuffle of semi-independent regional military commanders announced
in January 1974, which seemed at first to have reestablished the
authority of the central, more civilian government. If Premier Chou
was "sitting on a volcano," in Peking, we may take it that the rest of
Asia was also in danger from an overspill of some new Chinese
upheaval which might bring more hotheaded revolutionaries or un-
principled militarists into power.

Visiting Iran in June 1973, China's Foreign Minister Chi P'eng-
fei, declared: "This country must strengthen its defense forces." He
meant, of course, against Russia. At the same moment, the present
writer was hearing a catalog of charges against the Soviets from a
Chinese official in Peking; they used "self-styled leftists and socalled
Communist Parties" to subvert other countries, and sent warships to
intimidate them. The Peking media regularly play up stories about
Soviet spies, and accuse Moscow of creating trouble in the Persian
Gulf, and carrying out "frantic military expansion" in the Indian
Ocean, and making an "open show of force" in the western Pacific.

During 1974, a new charge of huge arms sales to Latin America was made. The Soviets were said to have engaged in large-scale penetration in the political, diplomatic, and economic spheres in Latin America by capitalizing on the "sharpening contradictions between US hegemony and Latin American nationalism." In his speech to the UN General Assembly in April 1974, Vice Premier T'ang even asserted that the USSR, like the US, carries out "economic plunder and political interference," and creates "states within states," because "the joint enterprises it runs in some countries under the signboard of aid and support are in essence transnational corporations."

From the other side, *Pravda* describes the "base methods" by which Peking carries out subversive activities, forms pro-Maoist groups, and supports separatist tendencies in the countries which it seeks to turn into its tools, and so forth. The charges from both sides are substantially correct. As far as Australia is concerned, however, the climate of opinion is such that anyone who points to this uncertainty or suggests the need to build up deterrent forces in being—and in good time—is taken to be a crank or a supporter of the splinter right-wing Democratic Labor Party, which was decimated after the last election and is regarded with loathing or derision by the intelligentsia. This climate of opinion is reinforced by most of the media and by Academia, out of conformism and invincible ignorance. In the last analysis, it is the educational system which is the first line of defense, since it is supposed to produce literate and thoughtful citizens. As in many other countries, the system is turning out too many "students" who can scarcely express themselves in speech, much less in writing. Without really learning to think, they are at the mercy of unscrupulous symbol-manipulators, whether advertisers or political propagandists. Here again, the remedy is not simply to spend *more* money, as the propaganda of both parties in the 1974 election suggested, but to spend it properly. Though resources are going to be dangerously short in the Third World and even perhaps in highly developed countries like Australia, the area where a great deal can be done to make them go further is evidently in proper allocation, hence in ideas. Security, or at least the minimization of disaster, ultimately depends on the education of public opinion, and its abandonment of dotty doctrines that proliferated in the age of relative plenty, which is now coming to an end.

Appendix I

Major Facilities of External Great Powers in the Indian Ocean

Base	Purpose	External Power Concerned	Remarks
US Naval Communications Station *Harold E. Holt,* Northwest Cape, Western Australia	Defense communications station in US global communications system	US	The station is under the joint operational control of the US Navy and Australia. The station cannot be used for other than defense communications without the agreement of the Australian government.
Asmara, Ethiopia	Military communications base, relay, and satellite tracking station in US global communications network	US	This base is now being run down.
Diego Garcia, BIOT	Naval communications center (part of global system), airfield, naval facilities	US/UK	Joint facility. Plans are to expand Diego Garcia into a permanent naval and air base.
Berbera, Somalia	Communications station	USSR	Function unknown.
Joint Defense Space Communications Station, Woomera, South Australia	A ground terminal for defense space communications involving satellites	US	The facility operated jointly with Australia.
Joint Defense Space Research Facility, Alice Springs, Northern Territory	To carry out a variety of defense space research functions	US	Jointly controlled by Australia and US.
Bahrain	Naval base for Mideast Task Force, communication station	US	
Massawa, Ethiopia	Port facilities for naval vessels	US	Serves Asmara base.
Vacaos, Mauritius	Tracking and telemetry, naval radio station, airfield	US/UK	Important observation post.

Appendix I
Major Facilities of External Great Powers in the Indian Ocean
(*continued*)

Base	Purpose	External Power Concerned	Remarks
Mahé, Seychelles	Communications station	US	Maintained by US Air Force.

Appendix II

United Kingdom, French, and Chinese Facilities in the Indian Ocean

Base	Purpose	External Power Concerned	Remarks
Gan Island, Maldives	Communications, airfield, RAF staging post, naval fuel supplies	UK	Earth station for Skynet.
Masirah Island	Communications, RAF staging post	UK	
Mahé, Seychelles	Airfield, harbor facilities	UK	
Mauritius	Harbor facilities	UK	
Djibouti, Territory of the Afars and the Issas	Airfield, harbor, radio station, military base, naval forces, air forces	France	Of great strategic importance if Suez Canal reopens.
Diego Suarez, Malagasy Republic	Naval base	France	To be evacuated by 1977.
Tananarive, Malagasy Republic	Air base, troops	France	Headquarters of French forces in the South Indian Ocean. To be evacuated by 1977.
Zanzibar, Tanzania	Telemetry for missile terminal ballistics	China	Existence speculative.

Appendix III

Other Defense-Related Establishments Operated by External Powers in the Indian Ocean Area

Base	Purpose	External Power Concerned	Remarks
US National Aeronautics and Space Agency tracking stations: Deep Space Station 41, Island Lagoon (Woomera), South Australia; Deep Space Station 42, Tidbinbilla, A.C.T. Carnarvon Tracking and Data Acquisition Station, Carnarvon, Western Australia; Honeysuckle Creek, A.C.T.; Space Tracking and Data Acquisition Network Station, Orroral Valley, A.C.T.; Applications Technology Satellite Station, Cooby Creek, Queensland; Baker-Nun Camera SC_{23}, Island Lagoon (Woomera), South Australia	Provide support for NASA's program of space exploration	US	Australia is responsible for the operation and management of the stations.
Tranet Tracking Station, Smithfield, South Australia	Support for the US geodetic satellite observation program on behalf of US Navy Pacific Missile Range	US	Australia is responsible for the operation and management of the station.
USAF Radio Receiving Station, Norfolk Island	Temporary station assisting the USAF in a research program involving the study of ionospheric propagation in relation to long-range radio paths	US	This station is at present operated by a contractor to the US government. Australia has the entitlement to participate in the work of the station.

Appendix III
Other Defense-Related Establishments Operated by External Powers in the Indian Ocean Area (*continued*)

Base	Purpose	External Power Concerned	Remarks
US Research Station, RAAF Base, Amberley, Queensland	Joint research program for the study of physical effects of disturbances in the atmosphere or space, with particular emphasis on radio communications	US	This station is managed and operated by the USAF. Australia has the entitlement to participate in the work of the station.
USAF Geological and Geophysical Research Station, Alice Springs, Northern Territory	Long-term geological and geophysical studies, including studies of earthquakes and attendant phenomena	US	This station is managed and operated at present by the USAF. Australia has the entitlement to participate in the work of the station.
US Geodetic Satellite Observation Program. Optical tracking stations (BC4 Cameras) at Culgoora, New South Wales, Perth, Cocos Island, Mawson, and Casey. A Doppler tracking system is in use at Smithfield, South Australia, SECOR stations at Darwin, Northwest Territory, and Manus Island. A BC4 camera is planned for Thursday Island, and a Doppler tracking system is planned for Heard Island	Temporary stations operated as part of the US geodetic satellite observation program	US	Operated by the US Army.

Appendix III
*Other Defense-Related Establishments Operated by External
Powers in the Indian Ocean Area (continued)*

Base	Purpose	External Power Concerned	Remarks
Trials Wing, Weapons Research Establishment, Salisbury, South Australia, and Missile Range and Support Facilities, Woomera, South Australia	Plan and direct firings and launchings at Woomera of missiles and vehicles under development as part of the UK/Australia Joint Project, or as mutually agreed for third parties, other countries, or international organizations	UK	The program is mutually agreed by Australia and the UK. Australia has sole control over the operation and management of the Trial Wing within the jointly approved program.
Joint Tropical Research Unit, Innisfail, Queensland	Exposure and storage of materials and selected military and other stores under tropical conditions, assessment of deterioration, and research into causes and prevention	UK	The program of the Unit is a joint responsibility with the UK Government. The Unit is under the operational direction of Australia.
Isle Amsterdam	Meteorological Station	France	Naval station
Crozet	Meteorological Station	France	Naval station
Kerguelen	Meteorological Station	France	Naval station
La Réunion	Relay Radio Station	France	

Bibliography

NOTE: The writer acted as Rapporteur to a series of conferences held by the Ditchley Foundation in 1966, and wishes to acknowledge his indebtedness to the participants for some of the points made in this essay. It also draws on material presented in a paper at the Eighth International Conference on World Politics held at Lake Yamanaka, Japan, in April 1973, and on my article published in *Art International—Lugano Review,* November 1973, under the title "Strategic Problems of the Indian Ocean Area."

Books and Reports

Alvin J. Cottrell and R. M. Burrell, eds. *The Indian Ocean, Its Political, Economic and Military Importance* (New York, 1972).

A. M. Jones. *Africa and Indonesia* (Leyden, 1964).

Devendra Kaushik. *The Indian Ocean, Towards a Peace Zone* (Delhi, 1972).

Colin Legum, ed. *Africa Contemporary Record* (London, 1969).

K. M. Panikkar. *India and the Indian Ocean* (London, 1945).

Parliament of Australia. Joint Committee on Foreign Affairs, *Report on the Indian Ocean Region* (Canberra, 1971).

Auguste Toussaint. *History of the Indian Ocean* (London, 1966).

UN General Assembly Ad Hoc Committee on the Indian Ocean. *Report of the Secretary General pursuant to paras 6 and 7 of General Assembly Resolution 3080 (XXVIII) 3 May 1974.*

US Congress. *The Indian Ocean: Political and Strategic Future.* Hearings before the Subcommittee on National Security Policy and Scientific Developments, Committee on Foreign Affairs, House of Representatives (Washington, 1971).

Monographs and Papers

W. A. C. Adie. *The Communist Powers in Africa* (London, 1970).

————. *China, Israel and the Arabs* (London, 1971).

————. *Chinese Stretegic Thinking Under Mao Tse-tung.* Canberra Papers on Strategy and Defense, No. 13 (Canberra, 1972).

American African Affairs Association. *The Indian Ocean Cockpit* (New York, 1971).

Geoffrey Jukes. *The Indian Ocean in Soviet Naval Policy.* Adelphi Papers, No. 87 (London, 1972).

T. B. Millar. *The Indian and Pacific Oceans, Some Strategic Considerations,* Adelphi Papers, No. 57 (London, 1969). *Soviet Policies in the Indian Ocean Area,* Canberra Papers on Strategy and Defense, No. 7 (Canberra, 1970).

Patrick Wall, *The Soviet Maritime Threat* (London, n.d.)

Journal Articles

In view of the number of topics and countries covered, only a sample can be given of the many articles that have been found useful. Space permits no citation of the many items used from Chinese, Soviet, regional and Western press and radio monitoring reports.

W. A. C. Adie. "Soviet and Chinese Policy in Asia," in E. Szozepanik, ed., *Symposium on Economic and Social Problems of the Far East* (Hong Kong, 1962).

————. "China's Middle East Strategy," *World Today* (August 1967).

————. "China Returns to Africa," *Current Scene* (Hong Kong) (August 1972).

————. "Peking's Revised Line," *Problems of Communism* (September/October 1972).

Center for Strategic and International Studies, Georgetown University. *The Gulf, Consequences of British Withdrawal* (Washington, D.C., 1969).

Ian Clark. "The Indian Subcontinent and Collective Security—Soviet Style," *Australian Outlook* (December 1972).

Government Information Department, Colombo, *Ceylon Today* (March/April 1971).

Christopher D. Lee. "Soviet and Chinese Interest in Southern Arabia," *Mizan* (August 1971).

D. P. O'Connel. "The Struggle for the Straits," *Quadrant* (August 1974).

Soedjatmoko. "China's External Policies: Scope and Limitation." Paper prepared for the 14th Annual Conference of the International Institute for Strategic Studies, Canada (September 1972).

Donald C. Watt. "The Decision to Withdraw from the Gulf," *Political Quarterly* (July 1968).

————. "Britain and the Indian Ocean," *Political Quarterly* (July/September 1971).

————. "The Persian Gulf: Cradle of Conflict?" *Problems of Communism* (May-June 1972).

National Strategy Information Center, Inc.

STRATEGY PAPERS

Edited by Frank N. Trager and William Henderson
With the assistance of Dorothy E. Nicolosi

Oil, Politics, and Sea Power: The Indian Ocean Vortex by Ian W. A. C. Adie, December 1974

The Soviet Presence in Latin America by James D. Theberge, June 1974

The Horn of Africa by J. Bowyer Bell, Jr., December 1973

Research and Development and the Prospects for International Security by Frederick Seitz and Rodney W. Nichols, December 1973

Raw Material Supply in a Multipolar World by Yuan-li Wu. October 1973

The People's Liberation Army: Communist China's Armed Forces by Angus M. Fraser, August 1973

Nuclear Weapons and the Atlantic Alliance by Wynfred Joshua, May 1973

How to Think About Arms Control and Disarmament by James E. Dougherty, May 1973

The Military Indoctrination of Soviet Youth by Leon Goure, January 1973

The Asian Alliance: Japan and United States Policy by Franz Michael and Gaston J. Sigur, October 1972

Iran, The Arabian Peninsula, and the Indian Ocean by R. M. Burrell and Alvin J. Cottrell, September 1972

Soviet Naval Power: Challenge for the 1970s by Norman Polmar, April 1972. Revised edition, September 1974

How Can We Negotiate with the Communists? by Gerald L. Steibel, March 1972

Soviet Political Warfare Techniques, Espionage and Propaganda in the 1970s by Lyman B. Kirkpatrick, Jr., and Howland H. Sargeant, January 1972

The Soviet Presence in the Eastern Mediterranean by Lawrence L. Whetten, September 1971

*The Military Unbalance
Is the U.S. Becoming a Second-Class Power?* June 1971

The Future of South Vietnam by Brigadier F. P. Serong, February 1971 (Out of print)

Strategy and National Interests: Reflections for the Future by Bernard Brodie, January 1971 (Out of print)

The Mekong River: A Challenge in Peaceful Development for Southeast Asia by Eugene R. Black, December 1970

Problems of Strategy in the Pacific and Indian Oceans by George G. Thomson, October 1970

Soviet Penetration into the Middle East by Wynfred Joshua, July 1970. Revised edition, October 1971 (Out of print)

Australian Security Policies and Problems by Justus M. van der Kroef, May 1970 (Out of print)

Detente: Dilemma or Disaster? by Gerald L. Steibel, July 1969 (Out of print)

The Prudent Case for Safeguard by William R. Kintner, June 1969

AGENDA PAPERS

Edited by Frank N. Trager and William Henderson
With the assistance of Dorothy E. Nicolosi